Fitness in the Elementary Schools

SECOND EDITION

Fitness in the Elementary Schools

A TEACHER'S MANUAL

Robert P. Pangrazi

Douglas N. Hastad

American Alliance for Health, Physical Education,
Recreation, and Dance
Reston, Virginia

Copyright © 1989
American Alliance for Health, Physical Education,
Recreation, and Dance
1900 Association Drive
Reston, Virginia 22091

ISBN 0-88314-426-3

About the Alliance

*T*he American Alliance for Health, Physical Education, Recreation, and Dance is an educational organization, structured for the purposes of supporting, encouraging, and providing assistance to member groups and their personnel throughout the nation as they seek to initiate, develop, and conduct programs in health, leisure, and movement-related activities for the enrichment of human life. Alliance objectives include:

1. Professional Growth and development—to support, encourage, and provide guidance in the development and conduct of programs in health, leisure, and movement-related activities which are based on the needs, interests, and inherent capacities of the individual in today's society.

2. Communication—to facilitate public and professional understanding and appreciation of the importance and value of health, leisure, and movement-related activities as they contribute toward human well-being.

3. Research—to encourage and facilitate research research which will enrich the depth and scope of health, leisure, and movement-related activities; and to disseminate the findings to the profession and other interested and concerned publics.

4. Standards and guidelines—to further the continuous development and evaluation of standards within the profession for personnel and programs in health, leisure, and movement-related activities.

5. Public affairs—to coordinate and administer a planned program of professional, public, and governmental relations that will improve education in areas of health, leisure, and movement-related activities.

6. To conduct such other activities as shall be approved by the Board of Governors and the Alliance Assembly, provided that the Alliance shall not engage in any activity which would be inconsistent with the status of an educational and charitable organization as defined in Section 501(c)(3) of the Internal Revenue Code of 1954 or any successor provision thereto, and none of the said purposes shall at any time be deemed or construed to be purposes other than the public benefits purposes and objectives consistent with such education and charitable status. *Bylaws, Article III*

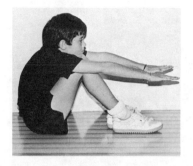

About the Authors

Robert P. Pangrazi has long been involved in studying the effects of physical activity on the growth and development of young children. He is Professor and former Chair in the Department of Health and Physical Education at Arizona State University and serves as a consultant to schools and universities throughout the United States. Author of many books and articles, Dr. Pangrazi has also produced six films on body movement education. He was technical director for *Bodytime,* an Emmy-award winning series on developing fitness in children that was nationally broadcast on PBS. As a concerned professional, Dr. Pangrazi is an active member of AAHPERD, a past president of the Arizona AAHPERD, and a former Executive Director of the Arizona Governor's Council on Health and Fitness.

Douglas N. Hastad is Chair of the Department of Physical Education and Associate Professor in the School of Education at Texas Christian University. Dr. Hastad served as Interim Dean for the School of Education from 1987 to 1988. He has taught at the elementary, secondary, university, and graduate school levels. He is author or coauthor of physical-education-related books and manuals, and has published articles in a wide variety of scholarly journals. He has also developed computer software packages, slide presentations, and audio tapes for use by physical educators. Hastad has conducted more than 100 workshops and presentations throughout the country on curriculum content for elementary physical education, health-related physical fitness for youth, and microcomputers in physical education and athletics, including major presentations at several recent AAHPERD national conventions.

Contents

CHAPTER THREE
Fitness for Special Populations   41

CHAPTER FOUR
Knowledge and Attitudes for Lifetime Fitness   51

CHAPTER FIVE
Fitness Activities and Routings   65

Preface

Fitness in the Elementary School is a book for teachers of children who are concerned about their physical fitness levels. Emphasis is placed on activities that are motivational and challenging to youngsters. In addition, a variety of activities are offered to assure that children will learn a number of methods for maintaining fitness.

Chapter One discusses the impact physical activity has on the growth and development of youngsters. It offers a rationale for including physical education in the school curriculum. Guidelines for exercising children safely are offered, including a new section on weight training for youngsters.

Chapter Two has been updated to include the new *AAHPERD Physical Best* fitness test. Also included is a new section offering guidelines for testing, measuring, and evaluating physical fitness. A comprehensive discussion is delineated explaining efficient test administration procedures and how to plan for fitness testing in the school setting.

Chapter Three focuses on special populations including obese and handicapped children. A new section discusses asthmatic youngsters, a common problem when fitness demands are expected. A number of suggestions for modifying activities to meet the needs of special populations are included.

Chapter Four takes a broader look at fitness, nutrition, substance abuse, and so forth, and the role they play in developing wellness in youngsters. Emphasis is placed on developing positive attitudes toward activity in order to stimulate lifetime fitness. Guidelines for leading wellness discussions are listed.

Chapter Five forms the heart of the book. This chapter is the focal point of the text and offers many activities for developing fitness in children of all ages. Effectively teaching a class in the fitness environment is discussed as is the importance of understanding the role of fitness in the total physical education lesson. An illustration of a yearly fitness program is included to help teachers plan a comprehensive approach to fitness. Finally, all the fitness activities have been field tested with youngsters. They work when teachers present them in a positive and enthusiastic manner.

Fitness in the Elementary Schools

CHAPTER ONE

Children and Physical Activity

*T*he primary purpose of this handbook is to offer a compendium of activities for developing physical fitness in children. However, fitness instruction involves more than presenting activities to youngsters. It is necessary to understand why fitness is important, how to develop fitness programs, and how fitness integrates into the wellness program. Following is a brief description of the contents in each chapter:

Chapter 1 gives background information on why physical fitness is important for the optimum growth and development of children. It also contains guidelines for assuring that the program is safe and within acceptable limits for youngsters. This chapter should be used as a basis of justification for the program when dealing with parents, administrators, and teachers.

Chapter 2 offers direction for developing a fitness program based on sound fitness principles. This chapter includes the new AAHPERD Physical Best fitness test, discusses the importance of self-testing, and offers methods of reporting test results to parents.

Chapter 3 deals with populations who need fitness, but find it difficult to find success—the obese, asthmatic, and handicapped. Direction for dealing with these students and adapting the program to meet their needs is offered. A section delineating strategies for modifying activities to assure the inclusion of all children is offered.

Chapter 4 emphasizes the importance of teaching physical fitness for a lifetime. It is important that physical education programs teach children how to maintain physical fitness independent of a teacher. Programs often emphasize "doing something to someone" rather than teaching individuals how to maintain personal fitness. Total fitness as part of a wellness program is discussed.

Chapter 5 contains many ideas, routines, and activities that can be implemented immediately to help improve the physical fitness of children in your classes.

This text is designed to be of immediate help in your instructional program. Bear the following in mind as you develop your program: **Physical fitness is a component of a well-rounded physical education program.** At no time should skill development and cognitive learning components be discarded for the sake of offering only physical fitness experiences to children. Without adequate physical skill and knowledge, students will lack the tools to participate in activities that can offer fitness development.

The Need for Physical Activity

An area of national concern is the lack of physical fitness among children. Recently, the President's Council on Physical Fitness and Sports issued a report showing that American youngsters showed no improvement, and in some cases showed a decline, in physical fitness since 1976. The school environment is not providing enough time and organized activity to develop an adequate level of fitness among its youth. Schools may be shortchanging youth in the area of health and wellness by refusing to offer physical education programs that offer emphasis and organization for health-related fitness development.

During the past decade, the interest in physical fitness and increased awareness of the benefits derived from an active life style have spawned a wide assortment of health clubs, a vast array of books and magazines concerning exercise and fitness, a weekly smorgasbord of distance runs and triathalons, streamlined exercise equipment, and apparel for virtually any type of physical activity. Unfortunately, most of this interest and life-style change has occurred among middle- and upper-class Americans. The truth of the matter is that very little change in fitness activity has occurred in lower middle- and lower-class families.

Unfortunately, the nation's enthusiasm for fitness and physical activity has not affected elementary school youngsters. A recent statement issued by the American Academy of Pediatrics reported that children from the ages of 2 to 12 watch about 25 hours of television per week, more time than they spend in school (Hastad, 1986). Only about a third of our children and youth participate daily (Ross, Pate, Corbin, Delpy, & Gold, 1987) in school physical education programs nationwide, and that number is both declining and insufficient. This compares unfavorably to the Surgeon General's 1990 goal of a 60% rate for physical education (U.S. Department of Health and Human Services, 1980).

The current status of children's physical fitness levels offers reason for concern. A report from the U.S. Department of Health and Human Services concluded that about half of American children were not developing the exercise and fitness skills to develop healthy hearts and lungs (Ross & Gilbert, 1985). In addition, concern was expressed that children were not developing a sound fitness base that would serve them throughout adulthood.

ARE CHILDREN NATURALLY ACTIVE? Children are not naturally active during a typical school day. Unfortunately, many adults observe children during recess, see a lot of children moving, and assume that they are extremely active. If they were to observe and follow individual children, they would see that children follow a pattern of moving and resting. Astute observers realize that children's play is characterized by long bouts of discussion, arguing, and questioning. A study by Gilliam, MacConnie, Geenen, Pells, & Freedson (1977), documented the fact that children do not voluntarily engage in high-intensity activity. By Gilliam et al.'s, definition, high-intensity activity occurred when the heart rate was elevated to at least 60% of its maximum. The children's heart rate was monitored to see how much time during a 12-hour period was spent in high-intensity activity. The results showed that less than 2%

of the children's time was spent in high-intensity activity, while 80% of their time was spent in low-intensity activity. Children do not receive enough fitness-enhancing activity during play experiences to develop an adequate level of health-related fitness. In addition to this finding, the researchers also found that girls were even less active than boys.

In addition, the study revealed that the school environment decreased the physical activity of children. Compared to summer activity, children's activity patterns decreased during the school year. Another interesting finding showed that if girls were given the opportunity, they would increase their activity levels to levels comparable to or above those of most moderately active boys. The authors concluded that daily activity patterns can be changed and coronary heart disease decreased through increased cardiovascular activity. This illustrates two points: (1) fitness does not occur through unorganized recess periods and (2) fitness improvement is possible for all children. This is a key point; physical fitness improvement can be accomplished by all, including boys, girls, and handicapped and obese children.

ARE CHILDREN FIT AND HEALTHY?

Heart disease is one area of concern when dealing with children's health. It has long been thought that heart disease is of geriatric origin and manifests itself only in older adults. In a study by Glass (1973), 5000 youngsters in the Iowa public schools were examined over a 2-year period. Of these students, 70% had symptoms of coronary heart disease, including 7% who had extremely high cholesterol levels; a large percentage had high blood pressure, and at least 12% were obese.

In examining the developmental history of heart disease in humans, Dr. Kenneth Rose (1973) identified the first signs as appearing around the age of 2. The good news is that he also determined that the disease process is reversible until the age of 19. Unfortunately, if children's exercise habits are not altered, they may be burdened with high blood pressure and/or obesity as they mature into adults.

According to Dr. John Kimball, a noted cardiologist at the University of Colorado, "evidence is growing stronger that the earliest bodily changes leading to heart disease begin early in life" (Albinson & Andrews, 1976). He also points out that more and more autopsy reports on children show blood vessels that have begun to clog with fatty deposits, which can eventually lead to heart attack.

Wilmore and McNamara (1974) examined 95 boys, aged 8 to 12 years, in an effort to determine the extent to which coronary heart disease risk factors derived from an adult population were manifested in a group of young boys. They concluded that "coronary heart disease, once considered to be a geriatric problem, is now recognized as being largely of pediatric origin."

There are other diseases associated with lack of activity in young children. One of the areas of grave concern is the high incidence of obesity among youngsters. Depending on the source of statistics and the criterion used to define obesity, anywhere from 30 to 60% of American children have been identified as obese. In addition, a lack of flexibility and upper body strength has been a recurring problem regardless of the source of testing and research. This lack often leads to poor posture and lower back pain in adulthood. The need is clear: develop healthy youngsters today who are capable of maintaining a healthy life style during adulthood.

The evidence points clearly to the fact that a large share of youngsters are not healthy. Although few children die of heart disease and related health problems such as obesity, there is a need for concern. For too long, parents and teachers have assumed that since children seldom complain about their health status, they are healthy. Physical educators owe children a legacy of personal fitness. A physical education program without a strong fitness component is taking away the only opportunity that children have to learn to maintain their health.

Exercise, Growth, and Development

Most adults are concerned about whether their child is maturing in a normal fashion. One of the quickest ways to stimulate the concern of parents is to invite them to observe their child in a physical education setting. If it appears their youngster is not performing on a level with other children, most will express immediate concern and ask what can be done to help the youngster improve. Following are some areas where studies have shown that exercise can impact the growth and development of children.

BODY PHYSIQUE   Exercise can impact, to some degree, a child's body physique. The child's physique also affects his or her performance in a wide variety of physical activities. Physical characteristics can be defined by somatotypes. The *mesomorph* is characterized as having a predominance of muscle and bone and is often labeled as "athletic and muscled." These children usually perform well in most team sports because the activities require speed, strength, balance, and agility. The *endomorph* is characterized as soft and round with an excess of digestive organs. These are usually identified as obese children who tend to do poorly in skilled and aerobic activities. This type of child is usually at a disadvantage in all physical education activities and requires special attention (see Chapter 3). The other somatotype is the *ectomorph* who is identified as thin, bony, and lacking muscle tissue. This youngster may do poorly in team sport activities but could excel in aerobic activities such as distance running and cross-country running.

One of the reasons for examining the effect of activity on somatotype is to understand that a certain type of individual may be predisposed to certain types of activity due to the opportunity to find success. If fitness programs do not offer a balanced approach emphasizing all components of fitness, the endomorphs and ectomorphs are at a distinct disadvantage. The key point is that a child's somatotype offers a general indication of his or her predisposition to certain types of activity. Use this as a starting point for introducing and "selling" physical fitness programming.

SKELETAL GROWTH   Strenuous physical activity has a positive effect on skeletal growth. Vigorous activity improves internal bone structure to help make the bones more resistant to breakage. The bones also grow larger in diameter and increase in mineralization in response to activity. It is well known that inactivity causes demineralization and makes the bones more susceptible to breakage.

An interesting phenomena, which can have a positive effect on a child's skill performance level, is caused by physical activity. Vigorous activity appears to cause the bones to shape themselves in a fashion that is mechanically advantageous for muscle attachments (Rarick, 1973). This increased mechanical advantage may allow a child to perform physical challenges at a higher level in later years when sport activities are more meaningful.

MUSCLES: STRENGTH,   In the elementary school years, muscular strength increases linearly with
FIBER TYPE, AND   chronological age (Malina, 1980). This implies that one can expect an increase
CAPABILITY   in strength fitness scores due to growth. The relative strength of children is important when pairing them for cooperative activities. Many problems can be avoided if a student is paired with someone who is similar in height and weight.

The number of muscle fibers that an individual possesses is genetically determined. An increase in muscle size is accomplished by an increase in the size of individual muscle fibers. The size of the muscles is determined first by the number of fibers and second by the size of the fibers. It is important to understand that some children are genetically positioned to perform better in strength activities than others.

Skeletal muscle tissue contains fibers that are fast contracting [(fast twitch (FT)] and others that are slow contracting [slow twitch (ST)] (Saltin, 1973).

Most people inherit a 50–50 split; however, it can vary as much as 98:02 in outstanding athletes. The FT fibers are capable of bursts of intense activity but fatigue rapidly. The ST fibers are slow contracting and resistant to fatigue. This makes them well suited to aerobic activities that demand endurance for long periods of time. In contrast, the individual who is endowed with a high percentage of FT fibers would be capable of short bursts of intense activity that are typical of most team sport activities. This points out the need to understand that children do not arrive at school with similar capabilities. Even though they are similar in age, they are very different physically. This emphasizes the need to offer a wide variety of physical fitness activities so that children of all types will find success at one time or another.

STRENGTH AND MOTOR PERFORMANCE

A strong justification for physical fitness lies in the area of strength development. A study by Rarick and Dobbins (1975) identified factors that contribute to the motor performance of children. Strength in relation to body size was the factor that weighed most heavily on the motor performance of children. Youngsters who exhibit high levels of strength in relation to their body size are more capable of performing motor skills than those with lower levels of strength.

This is just one of the problems created by being obese. The more obese a child is, the less proficient he or she is in performing motor skills since it reduces his or her strength relative to body size. One can liken the situation to carrying a 30-pound bag of sand in a backpack and trying to perform various motor skills. Body fat is dead weight that serves to reduce motor performance. Obese children may be stronger than normal-weight children in absolute terms, but they are usually weaker when their strength is adjusted for body weight. This lack of strength also causes the obese child to perceive a strength-related task as more difficult than a normal-weight child might. Teachers must have understanding and empathy for obese youngsters; they often do not like to exercise but they also find exercise much more difficult.

PHYSICAL FITNESS ACHIEVEMENT AND SELF-CONCEPT

One of the best things about physical fitness is that every student is capable of showing improvement. When students can view their self-improvement in fitness development, it has a strong impact on their feelings of competency. In no other area is success and failure as obvious as it is in physical education. It is obvious when a youngster achieves in physical fitness. A strong relationship has been established between self-concept and achievement (Purkey, 1970). The relationship appears to be based on low ability in that people with low self-concepts do less well than would be expected based on their ability level. The low performance reinforces the poor self-concept and the cycle continues.

It is important that physical fitness experiences be arranged so that students are offered the opportunity to improve their level of performance. If workloads are set too high, the first experience is one of failure. Always arrange the dosage so all students in the class can experience success. If each student is allowed to perform at a level that is in line with his or her ability, improvement will occur and is almost guaranteed by growth and maturation. Successful experiences can be arranged and made visible to others who are important to the student.

Physical appearance has a strong impact on how people view each other. A study by Richardson and Emerson (1970) shows that youngsters who possess handicaps not well accepted by society have lower self-concepts than "normal" children. Physical appearance, regardless of ability level, may negatively influence a person's self-concept. When looking at body somatotypes, the muscular body receives the highest rating from students and the obese body the lowest (Caskey & Felker, 1971). Unfortunately, students identify obese students with more than physical attributes such as "stupid, dirty, lazy, and smelly." The only area in the total school curriculum devoted to physical fitness and appearance is physical education. If children do not receive meaningful help in developing physical fitness, they may lose all motivation to pursue and maintain an adequate level of fitness for a lifetime.

PHYSICAL EDUCATION AND INTELLECTUAL DEVELOPMENT

Physical educators have long attempted to demonstrate a relationship between physical education and intellectual development. However, according to Shephard (1984a), "strong proof is lacking." A study that has created much interest is the Trois Rivieres regional experiment (Shephard, 1984b). The study provides a well-conceived design for showing the contribution of added physical activity to the academic achievement of students throughout their primary school years. Gains in academic performance (in comparison with control group students) were statistically significant in Grades 2, 3, 5, and 6. The more active students received higher grades in French, mathematics, English, and science, despite a 13% reduction in the time available for academic instruction.

Later evaluation of the study (Shephard, 1984b) found that sixth-grade students who participated in provincewide examinations continued to perform better. These results appear to counter the objection that more physical education (and in turn more physical fitness) will result in poorer academic performance due to less time spent in the classroom. It is difficult to imagine how the "back to basics" proponents can argue for an increase in academic vigor at the expense of the opportunity to enhance physical fitness. Certainly there are no priorities higher than physical health; without it, one is incapable of being a productive human being.

Understanding the Physical Limitations of Children

It is important to have a clear understanding of children's physical limitations in order to establish reasonable goals. Closely allied to this understanding should be an inherent empathy; if children think they are incapable of performing certain activities, their actual physical limits are of little concern. If children are pushed to fitness in a manner that develops negative attitudes toward lifetime fitness, the battle has been won, but the war was lost.

AEROBIC CAPACITY

Aerobic capacity, all other factors being equal, determines the magnitude of an individual's performance in endurance-oriented activities. Aerobic power is closely related to lean body mass, which explains why obese children and girls are often at a disadvantage in endurance activities. As they mature, girls tend to show an increase in body fat and a decrease in lean body weight which causes a gradual decrease in aerobic capacity when values are adjusted by body weight (Bar-Or, 1983).

A point often raised by individuals who question endurance activities is whether training actually improves the aerobic capacity of children. The research results differ in that some studies have shown a significant increase while others have reported no improvement. It appears that, particularly in children under 10 years of age, aerobic power does not increase with training even though running performance improves. The reason for the improvement in performance is speculation; however, it is thought that children may become more efficient mechanically or may improve in anaerobic metabolism. The fact remains that children should participate in aerobic activities in order to develop meaningful fitness habits and an understanding that aerobic exercise may be the cornerstone of a lifelong fitness program.

Even though children exhibit a relatively high oxygen uptake, they do not perform up to this level because they are not economical in running or walking activities. An 8-year-old child running at 180 m per minute is operating at 90% of maximum aerobic power, while a 16 year old running at the same rate is only at 75% of maximum. This explains why children should not be expected to perform workloads similar to adolescents, particularly over long distances. Youngsters can run long, slow distances at a slow speed.

Children are blessed in that they perceive activity to be easier than do adults exercising at a similar level. The Rating of Perceived Exertion was administered at different percentages of maximal heart rate (Bar-Or, 1977) and revealed that children perceive exercise to be less strenuous than adults. The reason for this is unknown; however, much research has documented the rapid recovery rate of children and the fact that exercise does not demand as much of children as it does of adults. The point of application for teachers is that they should not determine workloads for children based upon their perceptions of exercise difficulty. For example, if a teacher is not in a well-trained state, he or she might perceive the mile run to be next to impossible. This might not be the case for many children in a class. The important point here is to take advantage of children's rapid recovery rate. Aerobic activity can be interspersed with restful stretching and nonlocomotor movements to extend the amount of time effectively devoted to physical fitness development.

SKELETAL SYSTEM   The effects of exercise on the skeletal system are well documented. Bones modify their structure and hypertrophy when stress to the bones is gradually increased. Exercise is often used to prevent bone deterioration in the elderly. The key question is whether too much exercise can harm the skeletal system. In healthy children, the positive effects of physical activity outweigh any negative effects. However, if workloads are too great (too much resistance or too many repetitions) the beneficial effects of training are negated and the activity can disturb normal growth. For example, Caine and Lindner (1985) found that the growth curve for height was disturbed in two-thirds of a group of young prepubescent children involved in high-level gymnastics training. Overuse injuries have been reported in children in two areas: stress fractures and tendon attachments that may fail if excessive stress is applied to them. Most of these injuries appear to occur due to a lack of sufficient time to heal after training stress has occurred. It appears that, in most cases, exercise is extremely beneficial to proper development of the skeletal system. Problems occur when excessive stress is placed on the individual without an adequate rest and recovery interval. Whereas regular exercise is important to proper growth, intense training on a daily basis is probably less than beneficial to youngsters. As usual, the watchwords are moderation, progression, and consistency.

BODY COMPOSITION,   *Body composition* refers to the varying amounts of muscle, bone, and fat within
OBESITY, AND   the body. The primary concern in children is that of excessive body fat. Over half
PHYSICAL ACTIVITY   of the fat stored in the body is stored in a layer just below the skin. This is the reason that skinfolds are used to estimate the amount of fat carried within the body. Depending on the criteria used to evaluate the ratio of fat, 25 to 35% of youngsters have been identified as being overfat or obese.

Obesity restricts children's motor performance. Studies of childhood obesity have produced some disturbing findings. Many obese people appear to have a decreased tendency for muscular activity. As weight increases, the impulse for physical exertion decreases further. As children become more obese, they find themselves in a cycle that appears to be out of control. In most cases, physical activity appears to be the crucial factor in dealing with weight control. In comparisons of the diets of obese and normal children, no substantial difference in caloric consumption was usually found. In fact, in some cases, obese children actually consumed less food than did normal-weight children (Corbin & Fletcher, 1968).

A lack of physical activity is common among obese children. In a study of ninth-grade girls (Johnson, Burke, & Mayer, 1956), those who were obese ate less but also exercised two-thirds less (in total time) than did normal-weight girls. An examination of children in an elementary school in Massachusetts (Johnson et al., 1956) revealed that children gained more weight during the winter when they were less active. Movies taken of normal-weight and overweight children (Corbin & Fletcher, 1968) demonstrated a great difference in activity level of the two groups, even though diets were quite similar.

Adults often make the statement; "Don't worry about excessive weight; it will come off when the child reaches adolescence." The opposite is usually true, however. Four out of five obese children grow into obese adults; however, 28 out of 29 obese teenagers become obese adults (Johnson et al., 1956). Children clearly do not grow out of obesity—they grow into it. Childhood obesity needs to be challenged at an early age, and this challenge must come from increased movement and activity.

Identifying whether obese children are less active due to genetic or environmental factors is difficult. In a study by Rose and Mayer (1968), 4- to 6-month-old babies were divided into groups based on their level of obesity. The most obese children had the fewest limb motions, expending only 20% of their total energy on physical activity. In contrast, the leanest babies expended 35 to 40% of their energy on physical activity.

Griffiths and Payne (1976) selected 4- and 5-year-old children for study based on their parents' level of obesity. At the time of the study, the children were of similar body composition. Children of obese parents were, however, less active and also ate less than did the offspring of leaner parents. If the behavior continued, these children of obese parents would probably become obese due to lack of activity. The children's personal activity habits will have to change if they are to avoid obesity.

OBESITY AND PERFORMANCE

As mentioned, obese children seldom perform physical activities on a par with leaner children (Bar-Or, 1983). In part, this is due to the greater metabolic cost of the obese child's exercise. Obese children require a higher oxygen uptake capacity to perform a given task. Unfortunately, their capacity is usually lower than that of normal-weight children, which means that they must operate at a higher percentage of their maximum capacity. This forces obese children to operate at a higher percentage of their aerobic capacity, so they have less reserve. The lack of reserve probably explains why these children perceive aerobic tasks as demanding and unenjoyable. Teachers should bear this in mind when they ask obese children to try to run as far and as fast as normal-weight children. The task is more demanding for the obese child.

Obesity takes a great toll on a child's aerobic power because of the greater metabolic cost of exercise. Obese children must perform at a higher percentage of their maximal oxygen uptake. Their maximal uptake values are often lower than those of lean children, which gives them less reserve and makes them perceive higher exertion when performing a task. These reactions contribute to the well-known perception among teachers that "obese children don't like to run." What is needed is understanding by teachers that the obese child is working harder and that workloads must be adjusted accordingly. Since the obese child is working harder than the normal-weight youngster, it is quite understandable that aerobic demands will not be similar. There is no acceptable premise, physiological or psychological, for asking all children to run the same distance regardless of ability.

Workloads should be based on time rather than distance. Undoubtedly, the most efficient runner will move farther than the obese youngster during a stipulated time period. However, this is expected when teachers follow the principle of individual differences. All children **do not and should not** have to do the same amount of exercise. Just as one would not expect kindergarten children to perform the same workload as fifth-graders, it is unreasonable to expect obese children to be capable of workloads similar to those of lean, ectomorphic youngsters.

Guidelines for Exercising Children Safely

MODERATION IN EXERCISE

As is usually the case, moderation is the best way to ensure that children grow up enjoying different types of physical activity. Moderate exercise, coupled with opportunities to participate in recreational activity, help to develop a lasting desire to move.

Educators are sometimes concerned that a child may be harmed physiologically by too much or too vigorous activity. To date, there is no evidence that a healthy child can be harmed through vigorous exercise. This does not mean that a child is capable of the same unadjusted physical workload as an adult. Evidence does indicate, however, that children can withstand a gradual increase in workload and are capable of workloads comparable to those of adults when the load is adjusted for height and size.

There was concern at one time that the large blood vessels do not grow in proportion to other body parts. This, it was theorized, placed the heart and the circulatory system under stress during strenuous exercise. Research has now established that fatigue causes healthy children to stop exercising long before any danger to health occurs (Shephard, 1984a). In addition, the child's circulatory system is similar in proportion to that of an adult and is not at a disadvantage during exercise.

EXERCISING IN WARM CLIMATES

It is important to be aware of problems that can arise from exercising children when the climate is hot, humid, or both. Children do not adapt to extremes of temperature as effectively as adults due to the following differences in physiology:

1. Children have a greater surface area/mass ratio than adults. This allows a greater amount of heat to transfer from the environment to the body, thereby increasing body temperature.
2. Since youngsters are not as efficient in movement as adults, they generate more metabolic heat.
3. Sweating capacity is not as great in children as in adults, thus their ability to cool the body is less.
4. Since children have a lower cardiac output, they are less efficient at conveying heat from the body core to the skin.

These physiological differences make it clear that children are at a disadvantage when exercising in hot and humid climates. The following guidelines are offered by the American Academy of Pediatrics Committee on Sports Medicine (1982):

1. The intensity of activities that last 30 minutes or more should be reduced whenever relative humidity and air temperature are above critical levels.
2. At the beginning of a strenuous exercise program or after traveling to a warmer climate, the intensity and duration of exercise should be restrained initially and then increased gradually over a period of 10 to 14 days to allow time for acclimatization to the effects of heat.
3. Before prolonged physical activity, children should be fully hydrated. Make sure water is available if the conditions are hot and/or humid and the exercise is demanding.

Children who are obese are at an even greater risk since they are unable to dissipate heat as efficiently as normal-weight children. Stone (1977) recommends that running be restricted to periods of 15 minutes and active games consume no more than 45 minutes when the temperature is in excess of 85 degrees and the relative humidity above 40%. The key is to go easy in the heat and gradually increase the workload.

DISTANCE RUNNING— HOW MUCH?

In most physical fitness programs, running forms the core of the cardiovascular endurance activities. In most cases, any running that is not competitive where children can pace themselves and walk if necessary is safe, assuming the factors discussed above are followed. The problems occur when running becomes a highly competitive situation. When is a situation competitive for children? Any time the teacher puts children in a setting where they are expected to win in order to receive positive feedback from the instructor and peers. Teachers often forget the tremendous pressure some children are under due to their strong desire to be accepted. The following statement from the American Academy of Pediatrics Executive Committee (1982) identifies some of the concerns teachers should understand:

> Lifetime involvement in a sport often depends on the type of early participation and gratification gained. Psychological problems can result from unrealistic goals for distance running by children. A child who participates in distance running primarily for parental gratification may tire of this after a time and quit, or the child may continue, chafing under the parental pressure. In either case, psychological damage may be done, and the child may be discouraged, either immediately or in the long run, from participating in sports. A prepubertal child should be allowed to participate for the enjoyment of running without fear of parental or peer rejection or pressure. A child's sense of accomplishment, satisfaction, and appreciation by peers, parents, and coaches will foster involvement in running and other sports during childhood and in later life.

Another view by the International Athletics Association Federation (IAAF) Medical Committee (1983) gives a similar perspective:

> The danger certainly exists that with over-intensive training, separation of the growth plates may occur in the pelvic region, the knee, or the ankle. While this could heal with rest, nevertheless definitive information is lacking whether in years to come harmful effects may result.

> In view of the above, it is the opinion of the committee that training and competition for long-distance track and roadrunning events should not be encouraged. Up to the age of 12, it is suggested that not more than 800 meters should be run in competition. An increase in this distance should be introduced gradually—with, for example, a maximum of 3000 meters in competition for 14 year olds.

This suggested policy might be questioned by some who feel that it is in conflict with the mile run in the AAHPERD Fitness Tests. The IAAF statement speaks to high-level competition which involves intensive prerace training. The mile run test is offered as a form of self-competition and participants are offered the option of walking when necessary.

WEIGHT TRAINING

Weight training for preadolescent children has generated a great deal of concern among educators. Many worry about safety and stress-related injuries, and others question whether such training can produce significant strength gains. For some time, accepted thinking has been that prepubescents are incapable of making significant strength gains because they lack adequate levels of circulating androgens. Research evidence that contradicts this point of view is continuing to build. A study by Cahill (1986) demonstrated significant increases in strength among 18 prepubescent boys. A study by Servedio et al. (1985) showed significant strength gains in shoulder flexion. The results of these studies show that strength can be increased through weight training in prepubescent youngsters.

Note that the term *weight training* is used here to denote the use of barbells, dumbbells, or machines as resistance. It is in sharp contrast to *weight lifting* (and/or *power lifting*), which is a competitive sport designed to determine maximum lifting ability. There is strong agreement among experts that weight training is acceptable for children, but weight lifting is highly undesirable and may be harmful. In a statement of strength training recommendations, the American Orthopaedic Society for Sports Medicine (AOSSM) (Duda, 1986) states: "(1) competition is prohibited, and (2) no maximum lift should ever be attempted." In addition, AOSSM recommends a physical exam, proper supervision by knowledgeable coaches, and emotional maturity on the part of the participating youngster. Obviously, safety and prevention of injury are primary concerns for those interested in weight training for children. Serious thought must be given to whether weight training is an appropriate activity for a typical group of children in a physical education class. When injuries were reported, most occurred due to inadequate supervision, lack of proper technique, or competitive lifting. If knowledge and expertise in weight training are limited, these programs for children should be avoided. It takes a knowledgeable instructor to provide an effective and safe program.

There are no studies that examine the long-term effects of strength training in children. In addition, many experts worry about highly organized training programs that place great emphasis on relative gains in strength. A weight training program should be only one component of a comprehensive fitness program for children. The National Strength and Conditioning Association (1985) recommends that 50 to 80% of the prepubescent athletes' training include a variety of different exercises such as agility exercises (e.g., basketball, volleyball, tennis, tumbling) and endurance training (e.g., distance running, bicycling, swimming).

If a decision is made to develop a weight training program for children, it should be done in a thoughtful and studied manner. Proper supervision and technique are key ingredients in a successful program. Program prescriptions recommended by AOSSM and NSCS are:

1. Training is recommended two or three times a week for 20- to 30-minute periods.
2. No resistance should be applied until proper form is demonstrated. Six to fifteen repetitions equal one set; one to three sets per exercise should be done.
3. Weight or resistance is increased in 1- to 3-pound increments after the prepubescent does 15 repetitions in good form.

Fitness for a Lifetime

A guiding principle for teaching lifetime fitness is to make sure children are allowed the opportunity to make decisions about their capabilities. Too often instructors "do something" to children without allowing the youngsters' input. This process does little to help children understand their strengths and weaknesses and may cause a great deal of frustration. The days of a "daily dozen calisthenics and run a mile" must go the way of the dinosaur. There are many paths to fitness and each individual must be allowed the opportunity to discover the approach that works best for him or her. If people are expected to exercise for a lifetime, they must learn activities they enjoy and find beneficial.

This is not to suggest that the physical fitness experiences should not be demanding. It is to suggest that a youngster's feelings and self-worth should be considered at all cost. Fitness instructors must continue to emphasize the importance of nurturing and supporting students rather than embarrassing or belittling them when they find it impossible to measure up to an instructor's expectations. Youngsters find it very difficult to separate the behavior of the instructor from the content of the course. If they don't like the teacher, they probably won't like the subject matter, which necessitates that the instructor develop positive relationships with students if positive feelings toward physical fitness are to be developed.

In summary, instructors must be demanding and expect youngsters to perform. Educators have long understood that people will, to some degree, live up to expectations others have of them. Certainly, students should not be misled into believing that fitness is a relatively easy process. Fitness demands hard work and self-discipline and students should understand the process clearly. On the other hand, teachers should live up to expectations students have about them— that they are fair, understand individual differences, and care about the feelings and needs of students. Teachers who lead students to goals thought unattainable are true heroes!

References

Albinson, J. G., & Andrews, G. M. (1976). *Children in Sport and Physical Activity.* Baltimore: University Park Press.

American Academy of Pediatrics. (1982). Climatic health stress and the exercising child. *The Physician and Sportsmedicine, 11*(8), 155–159.

American Academy of Pediatrics. (1982). Risk in long-distance running for children. *The Physician and Sportsmedicine, 10*(8), 82–86.

Bar-Or, O. (1977). Age-related changes in exercise perception. In G. Borg (Ed.), *Physical Work and Effort.* New York: Pergamon Press.

Bar-Or, O. (1983). *Pediatric Sports Medicine for the Practitioner.* New York: Springer-Verlag.

Cahill, B. R. (1986). Prepubescent strength training gains support. *The Physician and Sportsmedicine, 14*(2), 157–161.

Caine, D. J., & Lindner, K. J. (1985). Overuse injuries of growing bones: The young female gymnast at risk? *The Physician and Sportsmedicine, 13*(12), 51–64.

Caskey, S. R., & Felker, D. W. (1971). Social stereotyping of female bodyimage by elementary school age girls. *Research Quarterly, 42,* 251–255.

Corbin, C. B., & Fletcher, P. (1968). Diet and activity patterns of obese and non-obese elementary school children. *Research Quarterly, 39*(4), 922.

Duda, M. 1986. Prepubescent strength training gains support. *The Physician and Sportsmedicine, 14*(2), 157–161.

Gilliam, T. B., Katch, V. L, Thorland, W. G., & Weltman, A. W. (1977). Prevalence of coronary heart disease risk factors in active children, 7 to 12 years of age. *Medicine and Science in Sports, 9*(1), 21–25.

Gilliam, T. B., MacConnie, S. E., Geenen, D. L., Pells III, A. E., & Freedson, P. S. (1982). Exercise programs for children: A way to prevent heart disease? *The Physician and Sportsmedicine, 10*(9), 96–108.

Glass, W. (1973). Coronary heart disease sessions prove vitally interesting. *California CAHPER Journal,* May/June, 7.

Griffiths, M., & Payne P. R. 1976. Energy expenditure in small children of obese and non-obese parents. *Nature, 260,* 698–700.

Hastad, D. N. (1986). Physical fitness for elementary school children. *Educational Theory, 1,* 12–14.

International Athletics Association Federation (IAAF). (1983). Not kid's stuff. *Sports Medicine Bulletin, 18*(1), 11.

Johnson, M. L., Burke, B. S., & Mayer, J. (1956). The prevalence and incidence of obesity in a cross section of elementary and secondary school children. *American Journal of Clinical Nutrition, 4*(3), 231.

Malina, R. M. (1980). Growth, strength and physical performance. In G. A. Stull & T. K. Cureton (Eds.), *Encyclopedia of Physical Education, Fitness, and Sports.* Salt Lake City UT: Brighton.

National Strength and Conditioning Association. (1985). Position paper on prepubescent strength training. *National Strength and Conditioning Association Journal, 7*(4), 27–31.

Purkey, W. W. (1970). *Self-Concept and School Achievement.* Englewood Cliffs, NJ: Prentice-Hall.

Rarick, L. G. (Ed.). (1973). *Physical Activity, Human Growth and Activity. New York: Academic Press.*

Rarick, L. G., & Dobbins, D. A. (1975). Basic components in the motor performances of children six to nine years of age. *Medicine and Science in Sports, 7*(2), 105–110.

Richardson, S. A., & Emerson, P. (1970). Race and physical handicaps in children's preference for other children. *Human Relations, 23,* 31–36.

Rose, K. (1973). To keep people in health. *Journal of the American College Health Association, 22,* 80.

Rose, H. E., & Mayer, J. (1968). Activity, calorie intake, fat storage and the energy balance of infants. *Pediatrics, 41,* 18–29.

Ross, J. G., & Gilbert, G. G. (1985). The National Council on Youth Fitness Study: A summary of the findings. *Journal of Physical Education, Recreation, and Dance, 56*(1), 45–50.

Ross, J. G., Pate, R. R., Corbin, C. C., Delpy, L. A., & Gold, R. S. 1987. What is going on in the elementary physical education program? *Journal of Physical Education, Recreation, and Dance, 58*(9), 78–84.

Saltin, B. (1973). Metabolic fundamentals of exercise. *Medicine and Science of Sports, 5,* 137–146.

Servedio, F. J., Bartels, R. L., Hamlin, R. L., et al. (1985). The effects of weight training, using Olympic style lifts, on various physiological variables in prepubescent boys. Abstracted. *Medicine and Science in Sports and Exercise, 17,* 288.

Shephard, R. J. (1984a). Physical activity and child health. *Sports Medicine, 1,* 205–233.

Shephard, R. J. (1984b). Physical activity and "wellness" of the child. In R. A. Boiliau (Ed.), *Advances in Pediatric Sport Sciences.* Champaign IL: Human Kinetics Publishers.

Stone, W. J. (1977). Running and running tests for Arizona School Children. *Arizona Journal of Health, Physical Education, and Recreation, 21*(1), 15–17.

U.S. Department of Health and Human Services. (1980). Promoting Health/Preventing Disease: Objectives for the Nation. Washington DC: U.S. Government Printing Office.

Wilmore, J. H., & McNamara, J. J. (1974). Prevalence of coronary disease risk factors in boys, 8 to 12 years of age. *Journal of Pediatrics, 84,* 527–533.

CHAPTER TWO

Implementing Physical Fitness Programs in Schools

*T*he many manifestations of active ways demonstrated by middle-class Americans may be misleading. Slowly, but effectively, the American public has been lulled into a false sense of security about the overall fitness levels in our country. The "fitness boom" may be a "fitness bust." Nowhere has this misrepresentation of adequate physical fitness been more evident than in American children. The most current national youth fitness study demonstrated that youngsters in Grades 5 through 12 were becoming fatter and were not achieving the minimum appropriate physical activity needed to maintain effectively functioning cardiorespiratory systems (Ross & Gilbert, 1985). The nation's burgeoning enthusiasm for fitness and physical activity has not trickled down to elementary school youngsters.

While statistics profiling the fitness level of children are alarming, physical education in the elementary school is at a crossroads. Responding with programs that place a renewed emphasis on physical fitness development, maintenance, and knowledge acquisition, elementary physical education has an opportunity to offset this deterioration of children's physical fitness. By capitalizing on society's request for physically fit youth, physical education can solidify and make more central its position in a child's total educational experience.

The following sections are intended to provide information that will aid the practitioner in understanding physical fitness, planning for fitness, developing fitness, measuring and evaluating health-related physical fitness, reporting assessment results, and promoting fitness.

Understanding Physical Fitness

Physical fitness is an important part of the normal growth and development of children. Physical education professionals and the AAHPERD Board of Governors (AAHPERD, 1988) define fitness as a state of well-being that allows people to (1) perform daily activities with vigor, (2) reduce their risk of health problems related to lack of exercise, and (3) establish a fitness base for participation in a variety of physical activities. This definition of fitness is rapidly becoming endorsed by various health and medical associations and better understood by the American public.

Teachers should examine how the physical education program communicates the importance of fitness to children. Attention should be given to providing learning experiences that focus on understanding and developing fitness. This communicates to children that fitness is an important aspect of a healthy and enjoyable life style. In fact, values shared with children should develop the comprehension that physical fitness is the foundation of skill performance, personal health, and wellness.

Through empirical research and scholarly inquiry, it is becoming increasingly clear that the multidimensional characteristics of physical fitness can be divided into two areas—health-related physical fitness and skill-related physical fitness. This clear differentiation between *physical fitness related to functional health* and *physical performance related primarily to athletic ability* has come about only after much discussion and debate. While this definitional distinction has curricular implications, classifying fitness into two categories should not lessen the importance of either in the total growth and development of youngsters. Understanding the distinctive features of the various components comprising health-related and skill-related physical fitness will assist educators in developing objectives and goals and planning learning experiences for elementary physical education.

SKILL-RELATED PHYSICAL FITNESS

Skill-related fitness includes those physical qualities that enable a person to perform a sport better. Synonymous with skill fitness is athletic fitness or general motor ability. The specific components that comprise skill-related fitness are agility, balance, coordination, power, and speed. Skill-related fitness components are useful in performing motor tasks related to sport and can be measured by a variety of test batteries that have been designed to assess and evaluate children's general motor ability. Most measurement and evaluation texts contain brief descriptions of appropriate tests and are valuable resources in the planning and administration of skill-related fitness tests (Hastad & Lacy, 1989).

Agility

Agility is the body's ability to rapidly and accurately change position while moving in space. Wrestling and football are examples of sports that require agility.

Balance

Balance refers to the body's ability to maintain a state of equilibrium while remaining stationary or moving. Maintaining balance is essential to all sports, but is especially important in the performance of gymnastic activities.

Coordination

Coordination is the ability to smoothly and successfully perform more than one motor task at the same time. Needed for football, baseball, tennis, soccer, and other sports that require hand-eye and foot-eye skills, coordination can be developed by continuously practicing the skill to be learned.

Power

Power is the ability to explosively transfer energy into force. To develop power, a person must practice activities that improve strength, but at a faster rate that involves sudden bursts of energy. Skills requiring power include high jumping, long jumping, shot-putting, throwing, and kicking.

Speed

Speed is the ability of the body to perform movement in a short period of time. Usually associated with running forward, speed is essential for the successful performance of most sports and general locomotor movement skills.

HEALTH-RELATED PHYSICAL FITNESS

Health-related physical fitness includes those aspects of physiological function that offer protection from diseases resulting from a sedentary life style. It can be

Table 2-1 Suggested Activities to Improve Skill-Related Physical Fitness

Component	Activities
Arm and shoulder girdle strength	Pull-ups, variations of the pull-up, rope climbing (hands only), and selected animal walks
Abdominal strength and endurance	Sit-ups, variations of the sit-up, selected animal walks, bending, stretching, and twisting
Agility	Selected stunts, zigzag run, selected sports skills
Leg power	Treadmill, vertical jumping, running, and standing long jump
Speed	Tortoise and Hare, running in place, selected leg exercises
Coordination	Locomotor movements, selected object manipulation skills, and most sports skills
Balance	Movements on benches or balance beam, selected balance stunts, and nonlocomotor tasks

improved and/or maintained through properly directed physical activity. Specific components include aerobic capacity, body composition (ratio of leanness to fatness), flexibility, and muscular strength and endurance. These components can be measured by the AAHPERD *Physical Best Fitness Education and Assessment Program* (AAHPERD, 1988) and are essential in developing and maintaining the physical health and well-being of children.

Aerobic Capacity

Aerobic capacity is the ability to exercise the entire body for extended periods of time without undue fatigue. A strong heart is necessary to effectively supply oxygenated blood to the muscles. In fact, aerobic fitness is essential for living a healthy day-to-day life and may be the most important element of fitness.

The greatest single cause of death in the United States is coronary heart disease. The annual percentage rate of Americans who die as a result of cardiovascular disease is greater than in any other country in the world. Ironically, coronary heart disease can be predicted by a person's life style. Several identifiable life-style habits associated with the onset on heart disease include stress, cigarette smoking, consumption of fat, and lack of physical activity and proper exercise. The result of these unhealthy practices usually results in elevated blood lipids, hypertension, and disturbances in heart rhythms.

Since an alarmingly high number of young children have been found to possess risk factors associated with the onset of coronary heart disease, it is important to teach them that active life styles will reduce their risk of heart disease. Learning experiences (i.e., paced walking, jogging, biking, rope jumping, aerobic dance, and other continuous-movement sports) that are continuous and rhythmic in nature are examples of the types of activities that develop and promote a healthy heart.

Body Composition

Body composition speaks to the amount of body fat a person carries and is represented by a percentage calculated from specifically designed tests. This component of health fitness is best visualized as a division of the total body weight into two components: fat weight and lean weight (muscle, bone, and internal organs). For example, an individual with a total body weight of 100 pounds who has been diagnosed as 20% fat would possess 80 pounds of lean weight and 20 pounds of fat weight. A fit person has a relatively low percentage of body fat.

Body composition is most commonly determined by converting the thickness of selected skinfold measurements to a percentage of body fat. A skinfold test requires the use of a small instrument called a *caliper*. A properly trained individual can accurately measure a two-site skinfold in a matter of seconds. When compared to more sophisticated and time-consuming laboratory tests, this method is sometimes inaccurate. However, it is significantly easier to administer in a field-based setting to large groups of students and more readily accepted and understood by parents and school officials.

Obesity is an excessive accumulation of fat weight and has been linked with the onset of various health problems. For good health, the body should maintain a proper ratio of fat to lean weight. Results of recent research indicate that obesity is more prevalent among American youth than ever before (Gilbert & Ross, 1985). These statistics are even more frightening when you consider that obesity is associated with many risk factors linked to the onset of coronary heart disease, stroke, and diabetes. Practicing good dietary habits and burning excess calories through proper physical activity and exercise are essential to reducing the percentage of body fat. Since the health and well-being of an individual is dependent on body composition, children should learn about concepts and consequences in this area.

Flexibility

Flexibility is the range of motion available in a joint or a sequence of joints. Muscles, tendons, and ligaments tend to retain or increase their elasticity through stretching activities. People who are flexible are less subject to injury during physical activity, usually possess sound posture, and may have less back pain.

Most Americans will, at one time or another, encounter back pain due to weak musculature. Stressful daily routines further increase the strain on the back and make the problem worse. Lack of physical activity has been found to be a contributing factor to the onset of lower back problems and greatly reduces an individual's flexibility in the lower back and hip flexors.

Children need to develop good exercise habits that will increase the flexibility of the lower trunk and posterior thigh regions. Through stretching activities, the length of muscles, tendons, and ligaments can be increased. Static or controlled stretching (without bouncing) is the recommended method for increasing flexibility. It involves gradually increasing the stretch to the point of discomfort, backing off slightly to where the position can be held comfortably, and maintaining the stretch for an extended time. Many physical activities demand a wide range of motion to generate maximum performance.

Muscular Strength and Endurance

Strength is the ability of muscles to exert force. Endurance is the ability of muscles to exert force over an extended period of time. Maintenance of minimal levels of trunk and hip strength/endurance are important in the prevention and alleviation of lower back pain and tension.

Misalignment of the spinal column can be the result of weak abdominal muscles. Research has demonstrated that improving the muscular strength and endurance of the stomach muscles can decrease the incidence and severity of pain in the spinal area.

Performing daily tasks requires adequate levels of muscular strength and endurance of the arm and shoulder girdle area. Lifting, pulling, pushing, and carrying objects without undue fatigue or pain depends on muscular strength and endurance of the upper body. Youngsters may also require upper arm strength to protect themselves in emergency situations.

Providing children opportunities to develop and maintain muscular strength and endurance of the abdominal, upper arms, and shoulder region is a vital part of a regular physical education program. Muscular endurance is probably best achieved using a low-resistance, high-repetition workload. There are many activities (animal walks, specific exercises, selected movement activities, and so on) that can be used with children to achieve this goal. Usually, muscular strength and endurance workouts should be conducted three days per week, which gives the muscles a chance to recover from exercise-induced stress.

Table 2-2 Suggested Activities to Improve Health-Related Physical Fitness

Component	Activities
Cardiovascular fitness	Jogging, cross-country skiing, walking, continuous rope-jumping, bicycling, swimming, and aerobic dance
Body composition	(same as Cardiovascular fitness)
Abdominal strength and endurance	Sit-ups, variations of the sit-up, selected animal walks, stretching and twisting
Flexibility of lower back	Bending and stretching, sitting stretch, partner stretching, and selected animal walks
Arm and shoulder strength and endurance	Pull-ups, rope climbing (without using legs), push-ups, selected animal walks, and most climbing activities

Planning for Physical Fitness

A broad program for physical education requires that children develop a level of health related physical fitness commensurate with their need and acquire an understanding of the concepts associated with fitness development. Through exciting learning experiences and encouragement from the teacher, it is also hoped that youngsters will develop sufficient interest to voluntarily participate in physical activity. Improving fitness, teaching the children the why of fitness, and having students select physical activity as part of their life style are best accomplished through proper planning and a balanced program of physical fitness. Learning activities that address each of these three objectives should be incorporated into the daily lesson. The following sections describe ways in which this can be accomplished.

IMPROVING PHYSICAL FITNESS

A fitness development program should be part of each lesson. Organized routines that develop total fitness should be presented in an exciting manner. Youngsters should look forward to participating in this phase of the lesson. This component of the lesson should be varied every 2 weeks and consist of activities and/or exercises that develop the various elements of health-related physical fitness. The exercise routine should be approximately 8 to 12 minutes in duration and allow sustained activity for all children in class. Chapter 5 details examples of routines that are appropriate for this phase of the lesson.

TEACHING THE WHY OF PHYSICAL FITNESS

When introducing fitness routines, it is appropriate to explain basic anatomical or physiological points associated with performance of the exercises. Children should learn the names and locations of major bones and muscle groups, including how they function in relation to selected joint action. Information presented should relate to fitness actions appropriate to the students' developmental level. Youngsters also need to be made aware of the values derived from maintaining minimal levels of physical fitness. To accomplish this, the teacher must devote time to explaining the basic features of a personal fitness program for life.

PROMOTING PHYSICAL FITNESS

Students should learn that, ultimately, it is their responsibility to develop personal fitness. Youngsters should be helped in setting and achieving personal fitness goals that have meaning. Attaining realistic goals will encourage further participation and serve to motivate youngsters to voluntarily take part in sports and physical activity. Establishing planned fitness activities that extend beyond normal school hours can aid in promoting fitness. For example, jogging clubs, aerobic dance classes, swimming programs, and biking activities can be conducted before or after school hours and serve to provide additional fitness opportunities for children.

Developing Physical Fitness

Positive changes in physical fitness result from participation in exercise routines that adhere to principles of exercise. Developmental experiences that address all components of fitness and comply with principles of exercise should be included as a separate portion of the physical education lesson. Chapter 5 details fitness routines and exercises that can be incorporated into the daily lesson.

GUIDELINES FOR DEVELOPING PHYSICAL FITNESS

If we want children to be physically fit and adopt a physically active life style, educational experiences must be broad and well planned. There is much more to developing and maintaining physical fitness in children than just including exercise as part of the program. Physical fitness is not a byproduct of physical education, a chance occurrence, or a commodity measured only by performance scores. Children should acquire the basic concepts of fitness, learn the value of regular exercise and begin taking responsibility for their own physical well-being, and, of course, regularly experience vigorous physical activity. A balanced approach toward fitness experiences is essential if fitness is to be extended beyond the confines of the gymnasium.

Teachers must follow selected principles of exercise if the physical fitness levels of children are to be improved and maintained.

Frequency, Intensity, Time (FIT)

The acronym FIT can be used to remember the three most important principles of exercise: frequency, intensity, and time.

Frequency refers to regularity of exercise. The number of days per week a youngster is involved in vigorous physical activity is used to determine frequency. Children should be involved in vigorous physical activity 3 to 5 days per week.

Intensity refers to how much effort is expended during exercise. The method of determining intensity depends on the component of fitness exercised. For instance, cardiovascular effort is measured by heart rate, the degree of above-normal exertion indicates how hard muscles are working, and distances of beyond-normal stretching are used to measure intensity of flexibility activities. Fitness benefits can be derived when children work at 60 to 90% of their working heart rate. Table 2-3 shows suggested exercise target heart rates for children.

Table 2-3 Estimates of Threshold Target Heart Rate for Children

Resting Heart Rate	Threshold or 60% of Working Hr.
Below 60	150
60–64	151
65–69	153
70–74	155
75–79	157
80–84	159
85–89	161
90 and Over	163

Time refers to the length of the exercise period. Usually measured in minutes, this time of exercise involvement is also referred to as *exercise duration*. The fitness modules described in Chapter 5 can be varied to accommodate the length of the time period available for fitness development. Ten to fifteen minutes of sustained vigorous activity (including warm-up) is the recommended minimum time for an exercise period.

Other principles of exercise to be considered when structuring fitness routines are progression, warm-up, mode of activity, specificity, and initial level of fitness.

Progression   Progression refers to the sequencing of exercise and usually involves manipulation of FIT to prevent some of the negative aspects often occurring with fitness activities. Muscle soreness and the early onset of fatigue due to lack of continuous vigorous activity may cause children to balk at high-intensity activity. Since it is common for a child's level of physical fitness to deteriorate during the summer months (if fitness has been developed during the school year), fitness routines for the first several weeks of school should be reduced in intensity and progressively increased thereafter. If there is a need for additional energy expenditure, the frequency and time factors can be increased accordingly. In school programs where frequency and time may be limited, a gradual increase in intensity is the only alternative. There is little evidence available outlining a "best" implementation strategy for progression. A general recommendation would be to increase the work load by no more than 10% per week. Whatever the case, a conservative approach is the best method of fostering a positive attitude toward exercise that will last a lifetime.

Warm-up   Warm-up is an initial period of physical activity that prepares the youngsters for the vigorous exercise to follow. Proper warm-up and stretching may help prevent muscle and joint soreness and give the respiratory and circulatory systems a chance to adapt. Activities should be unstructured (i.e., no new skills are introduced) and consist of gross movements that utilize the large muscle groups. This gradual progression into activity makes the children more comfortable as they get ready for the more intense phase of the lesson.

Mode of Activity   Mode of activity describes the types of activity that are conducive to fitness development. It is important to remember that any activity that can be adapted to comply with FIT standards is appropriate. The most common fitness activities are jogging, general exercise, walking, swimming, bicycling, cross-country skiing, and aerobic dance. Chapter 5 details specific fitness routines for children.

Specificity   Specificity refers to developing a particular component of fitness through specifically designed exercises of proper FIT. For example, if the desired outcome is improved abdominal strength, then the exercise(s) selected must work the abdominal muscles. The specificity principle means that it is essential to carefully plan fitness routines that will elicit the desired alterations in fitness. Exercises to develop specific components are described in Chapter 5.

Initial Level of Fitness   Initial level of fitness refers to the variation of fitness exhibited by children. The continuum of fitness extends from those with low levels of physical dysfunction/disability to youngsters with high levels of physical function/ability. Strategies must be developed that offer children at both ends of the continuum opportunities to profit from the benefits of exercise without being discouraged or frustrated. Fitness activities must be individualized to accommodate the manipulation of intensity.

Testing, Measuring, and Evaluating Physical Fitness

Tests, measurement, and evaluation are becoming increasingly more important parts of a physical educator's responsibilities. Nationwide efforts are currently being initiated that will encourage the testing, measurement, and evaluation of the health fitness status of youth. The results of these large-scale campaigns are designed to provide quantitative information about the fitness level of youth and to educate students about the importance of maintaining physical fitness.

Practitioners are expected to conduct formal testing and evaluation of students. Rather than viewing this as an additional burden and "just one more thing to do," measurement and evaluation should be approached as mechanisms to assist the physical educator in being more effective. Teachers who are able to provide quantitative evidence showing progress toward stated goals will be in a position to negotiate for additional programmatic resources. Those who ignore the importance of utilizing measurement and evaluation could place programs in serious jeopardy.

TESTING, MEASUREMENT, AND EVALUATION

Testing is an all-encompassing term that refers to instruments, protocols, or techniques used to measure a quantity or quality of properties or attributes of interest. In physical education, properties or attributes in areas such as cognitive knowledge, values, general motor ability, and components of health-related physical fitness are subject to testing.

Many types of tests can be effectively utilized in physical education settings. For example, a test commonly used to measure aerobic capacity is the mile run. This distance run can provide the instructor with a quantitative measure of the time it takes for an individual to complete a mile. This score can then be used to make additional judgments regarding the cardiovascular fitness of the subject.

Measurement is the process of collecting data on a particular attribute. Measurement should be as precise, reliable, and objective as possible. Results are normally expressed in some type of numerical form that indicates the quantity of the property or attribute being measured. For example, when the mile run is used as a test of aerobic capacity, the performance is measured by timing the trial. The recorded measurement would indicate the total time needed to complete the test. It is important to remember that an appropriate test must be selected and properly administered before any confidence can be placed in the final measurement. A valid and reliable test will yield inaccurate measurements if the administration of the test is conducted in a less than objective manner under varied conditions.

Evaluation is the process of interpreting the collected measurement and determining some worth or value. Many times, this interpretation of worth will be done by comparing results to predetermined criteria, or objectives. Without the availability of tests and the resulting measurements, the evaluative process would lack important information necessary for informed and impartial decisions.

In many instances, comparing the results of a test with other similarly obtained scores would allow valid comparisons. For example, comparing the results of a student's performance in the mile run with another like person who has completed the test under similar conditions would offer an opportunity to make evaluative decisions regarding the differences in aerobic capacity. Another way to evaluate results would be to compare scores against a predetermined standard or criterion.

Keep in mind that measurement is necessary for evaluation. Measurement represents the status of a certain attribute and is a terminal process. Evaluation is a broader term representing a more complex process and may be expressed in qualitative terms. Evaluation determines the extent that objectives are met and is an ongoing and continuous process. By comparing measurements to objectives, it is possible to form conclusions based on sound judgment and rational thinking to improve the quality of the physical education program.

FACTORS TO CONSIDER WHEN SELECTING A TEST

For a testing program to be effective, it is necessary to avoid the pitfall of selecting tests which, due to your particular situation, may be no more than logistical nightmares. A careless approach to test administration can result in invalid scores. Since the time involved with testing in physical education should consume no more than 10% of the total instructional time, it becomes only prudent to select tests that are compatible with various aspects of the overall program. Therefore, during the planning phases, the practitioner should consider several practical criteria before deciding on a test.

After acceptable validity, reliability, and objectivity of a test have been determined, it is the instructor's responsibility to identify factors that affect the efficiency and management of the testing program. Only after thorough deliberations about these factors should a test or testing program be considered for inclusion in the yearly program. The following are characteristics of tests that need to be considered before a final decision is made.

Economy

Tests should be economically feasible in terms of equipment and personnel. Since most of the budgetary allocations for physical education are spent on instructional equipment and supplies, it is imperative that test batteries require a minimal amount of financial expenditure. Tests selected should also allow for judicious use of personnel needed to administer the various phases of the test.

Time

Tests should be administered in a relatively short period of time. Remember, the great majority (approximately 90%) of the time in physical education should be devoted to learning experiences designed to meet predetermined goals.

Educational Value

The testing program should be a learning experience for the students. The process of test administration should communicate the importance of the components being measured and the relationship of these elements to the program objectives. Students should learn something about themselves and the qualities being assessed.

Enjoyment

Tests should be nonthreatening and a relatively enjoyable experience. Many individuals experience anxiety and apprehension before and during a testing session. Physical educators should take measures to ensure that the testing sessions are as enjoyable as possible and in no way discourage youth from participation in physical activity.

Norms

Tests should have normative data available to assist in the interpretation of scores. *Norms* are values representative of a particular population. Normative tables provide a way to compare student performance to a larger, yet similar, population. These comparisons can provide the teacher and student with valuable information about the relationship of individual performance scores to scores of similar age and gender youngsters.

Relevance

Only tests that measure criteria related to program goals should be administered. Tests must be relevant to both stated objectives and learning experiences. For example, selecting a test that measures various components of health-related physical fitness is only appropriate if the instructional program is designed and interested in developing health-related physical fitness.

Discrimination

Test results should discriminate among all students taking the test. A test should be able to take into account the wide range of performance capacities and abilities of students. It is recommended that test items be designed to measure the qualities of function that extend along a continuum from severely deficient to high levels of functional capacity.

Independence   A test battery should contain items that are valid measures of a particular variable, yet unrelated to other items in the test battery. Having students run the mile and the 12-minute run to measure cardiovascular fitness would be time consuming and provide a duplication of information. Each test item in a battery should measure a different quality or trait.

Sex Appropriateness   Tests should take into account the differences between males and females in such a way that the process does not bias in favor of one sex. In selecting and administering tests, teachers should be continually aware of the inherent differences between boys and girls. Administering tests with available norms allows the teacher to compare students' raw performance scores with normative scales of same-age and gender individuals. Comparisons to standards should take into account differences in performance attributable to gender.

Safety   Select tests that pose little, if any, risk to students that also can be conducted in a safe environment. Criteria to be considered in determining whether a test is safe include station site, the potential for students to overexert, and the capabilities of students. Most of the time, safe test administration means exercising good judgment and common sense.

Testing Large Groups   Tests that allow a large group of students to be tested in a relatively short period of time are preferred. With large classes, it is important that students be measured as quickly, yet accurately, as possible. This can be accomplished by testing students successively or simultaneously. Using the school nurse, other classroom teachers, aides, parents, or local college students can greatly reduce the time it takes to test a large number of students.

Ease of Scoring, Interpreting, and Reporting   A test should allow for easy and accurate scoring and be used as a self-assessment by students. Selecting tests that can be easily scored on specially designed forms or have accompanying microcomputer software for quick and accurate interpretation and reporting are time-saving considerations.

PLANNING TEST ADMINISTRATION   Once the test battery has been selected, planning for the testing session can commence. Proper planning increases the likelihood of efficient and uneventful test sessions. This, of course, increases the chances for obtaining valid, reliable, and meaningful scores. To be effective, a testing program requires good planning. Planning involves a number of specific tasks.

Securing Materials and Preparing the Testing Area   Proper use of space, equipment, and supplies reduces the amount of time required for test administration. Competent test administration begins with compiling a detailed list of test equipment, supplies, and other materials needed. Planning for appropriate utilization of space can reduce set-up time, assure a safer environment, eliminate confusion, and minimize crowding.

Know the Test   The test administrator should have a thorough knowledge of the test and a precise understanding of its administrative procedures. It is also helpful if students are familiar with the test items and understand the reasons for taking the test. Knowing the number of trials per test item, exact measurement techniques, and recommended organizational procedures associated with each test increases efficiency and improves accuracy of results.

Recording the Scores   The manner in which raw scores are recorded onto scorecards is integral to the efficiency of the testing program. Scoring forms should be designed and printed prior to the test sessions. In most cases, the instructor is responsible for devising the scorecard to be used for recording performance scores. In addition to a place to record the raw scores, these forms should include space for the student's name, age, height, weight, grade, homeroom, and teacher. Generally, a 5- by 8-inch index card provides sufficient space for all necessary categories. Figure 2–1 is an example of an individual scorecard for the AAHPERD *Physical Best* testing program.

School Year: _____ Classroom Teacher _____

Name _____ Age _____ Birthdate _____ Grade _____

| **Dimensions (opt.)** | **Fitness Test** |

Height _____

Weight _____

Body Mass Index _____

Mile Run/Walk _____ min. _____ secs. _____

Pull-ups _____

Sit-ups _____

Sit and Reach _____ cm. _____

Triceps _____ mm. _____

Calf _____ mm. _____

Sum of Skinfold _____ mm. _____

Lap Times Using 220 Yard Oval

Lap #1 _____ Lap #5 _____

Lap #2 _____ Lap #6 _____

Lap #3 _____ Lap #7 _____

Lap #4 _____ Lap #8 _____

Mile Run Time _____ In Seconds _____

Figure 2–1 Example of a Raw Data Card for the Physical Best Fitness Test

Train Testers
Test administrators should be efficient and accurate in testing students. It is recommended that practice sessions be conducted with a sample of subjects. These sessions can be used to clarify instructions, standardize procedures, and develop technical skills needed for successful test administration. The emergence of several new batteries of health-related physical fitness tests has prompted many schools and districts to devote inservice time to training teachers in the methods and procedures associated with test administration.

Practice Test Items
A primary source of measurement error is not allowing students the opportunity to become familiar with and practice test items. Reliability of results is increased if students are familiar with the test items. Students should also be informed well in advance of upcoming tests so that they can prepare. For example, if a distance run is forthcoming, students should understand the concept of pace, be aware of their optimal pace, and have experience in running for extended duration. Students should also be given ample time to develop some degree of physical fitness prior to taking a test that requires extreme physical exertion.

Warm-Up
Provide an initial period of 5 to 10 minutes for students to physiologically and psychologically prepare for test taking. Proper warm-up and stretching exercises may also help prevent muscle and joint injury that could occur as a result of maximum effort on the test. The warm-up is not only a safety precaution, it also improves performance on most tests.

Standardize Instructions
Directions should be prepared in written form. Caution must be taken so that some students are not given different or additional information about how the test should be completed.

Interpreting and Evaluating the Results
Interpreting scores enables the teacher and students to monitor progress toward goals and identify strengths and weaknesses. Another vital phase of the posttest procedure is the evaluation of scores in relation to the process and product. Follow-up evaluation usually results in the refocus of aims or goals of the program and an alteration in the delivery system used to attain stated goals.

AAHPERD *Physical Best: Fitness Education and Assessment Program*

Valid reasons for measuring children's physical fitness are numerous and varied. The testing and evaluation process is further complicated because of the abundance of test batteries devised to measure various components of physical fitness. Given the increased emphasis elementary physical education programs are placing on developing physical activity habits that last a lifetime, it seems timely to focus our attention on a test battery that measures components of health-related physical fitness. Valid and reliable results that can be accurately and meaningfully interpreted can be obtained by using *Physical Best: The American Alliance Physical Fitness Education and Assessment Program* (1988). Each element of health-related physical fitness is measured by one or more of the five *Physical Best* tests. This particular test battery is characterized by many of the traits that facilitate test administration and will provide students with an overall appraisal of their current health-related fitness status. The following sections briefly describe the features of *Physical Best* and provide a brief synopsis of each test item. Activities to improve fitness are more thoroughly explained in Chapter 5.

PHYSICAL BEST: A PHYSICAL FITNESS EDUCATION AND ASSESSMENT PROGRAM

Physical Best is a comprehensive physical fitness and assessment program designed for boys and girls 5 to 18 years old. It has been specially developed to encourage children and youth of all abilities, including the handicapped, to participate in physical activity for the purpose of achieving their personal best in physical fitness. This program combines assessment of health-related physical fitness with practical classroom instructional materials that teach the why and how of staying fit for a lifetime.

Three components comprise the complete *Physical Best* program: (1) a health-related fitness assessment, (2) an educational component, contained in a kit available from AAHPERD, and (3) a set of awards, to reinforce positive behavior change and recognize personal achievement. In this text we describe only the assessment portion of the program. A detailed explanation of the accompanying educational program can be found in Sections 1 and 3 of the *Physical Best* test manual (AAHPERD, 1988). This manual, as well as additional materials regarding *Physical Best*, can be obtained by writing directly to American Alliance, P.O. Box 704, Waldorf, MD 20601.

The assessment component of *Physical Best* contains five tests, each of which measures an element of health-related physical fitness. The components of health fitness and the techniques used to measure them are as follows:

- *Aerobic Capacity* is measured by the *One-mile Walk/Run*.
- *Body Composition* is measured by the *Sum of Two Skinfolds*.
- *Flexibility* is measured by the *Sit-and-Reach*.
- *Muscular Strength/Endurance* is measured by *Timed Sit-ups*.
- *Upper Body Strength/Endurance* is measured by *Pull-ups*.

The following description of these test items has been condensed from the *Physical Best: Physical Fitness Education and Assessment Program* (AAHPERD, 1988).

One Mile Walk/Run

Rationale

The importance of measuring cardiorespiratory fitness lies in the fact that heart disease is the leading cause of death in our society and risk factors associated with the onset of heart disease have been identified in children. Being able to assess and evaluate the functioning of the cardiovascular system through field

Figure 2-2 One Mile Walk/Run

tests is valuable in determining the type and amount of exercise needed to develop and maintain a strong heart and lungs.

Purpose
The purpose of the distance runs is to measure maximal function and endurance of the cardiovascular-respiratory systems.

Instructions
Students are told to run 1 mile in the fastest possible time. Walking is permitted, but since the objective is to cover the distance in the shortest possible time, students should be encouraged to run at the fastest pace they can sustain for the 1-mile distance.

Organizational Hints
(1) Using children in the intermediate grades (4-6) as lap counters and recorders can relieve the teacher of some administrative burdens and contribute to a positive running environment for youngsters in the primary grades (K-3). (2) Prior to engaging in the distance run test, children should receive ample instruction and practice in running for distance. (3) Particular emphasis needs to be placed on the concept of pace. (4) The purpose of the test should be explained to the youngsters, and steps should be taken to ensure a high level of motivation. (5) Children with known medical problems that would contraindicate vigorous exercise should be excluded from the test. (6) A warm-up period should immediately precede the mile run.

Test Area
Any smooth, flat area safe for running where distance can be accurately measured may be used for testing.

Equipment and Supplies
Stopwatch or watch with a sweep second hand, scorecards, and pencils.

Scoring
The time in minutes and seconds it requires to cover the 1-mile distance is the student's score.

**Sum of Triceps and
Calf Skinfolds**

Rationale
The reason for measuring millimeters of skinfold thickness is that it is the most reliable and valid field test to determine total body fatness. Regular monitoring of body fat can greatly assist the practitioner in structuring special exercise programs to meet the needs of normal and obese children. See Chapter 3 for a suggested program for obese children.

A *skinfold* is a double layer of skin and underlying fat. Two sites, the triceps and calf, have been chosen because each is easily measured and the sum of both is highly correlated with total body fat.

Purpose
The purpose of the skinfold test is to evaluate the percent of body fatness.

Instructions
The triceps skinfold is measured on the right upper arm, midway between the elbow and the shoulder. Grasp the double fold layer of skin between the thumb and index finger with the skinfold running vertically. Gently lift the skinfold with the thumb and index finger 1/2 inch above the midpoint of the arm and measure with the calipers (Figure 2-3). The calf skinfold is measured on the inside (medial side) of the right lower leg at the largest part of the calf girth. Grasp and gently lift the skin up slightly above the level of the largest part of the calf with the thumb and index finger so the calipers may be placed at the level of the largest part of the calf (Figure 2-4). Each skinfold site should be measured three consecutive times with the recorded score being the median (average) of the three scores.

Organizational Hints
(1) Practice in skinfold measurement is necessary to ensure reliable and accurate scores. (2) Proper technique includes accurately locating the site,

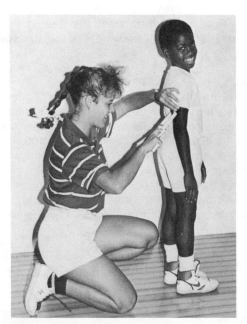

Figure 2-3 Triceps Skinfold

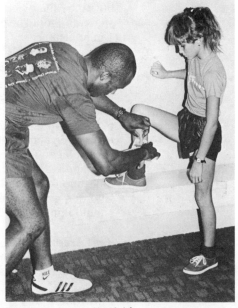

Figure 2-4 Calf Skinfold

firmly grasping the skinfold between thumb and forefinger and lifting it away, placing the caliper 1/2 inch below the skinfold, slowly releasing the pressure on the caliper trigger so that full tension can be exerted on the skinfold, and then reading the scale. (3) When measuring the calf skinfold, have students place their right foot on a bench with the knee slightly flexed.

Test Area

Any area free of distractions is suitable for administering the skinfold test.

Equipment and Supplies:

An accurately calibrated caliper is needed for taking these measurements; however, some of the less expensive plastic calipers are acceptable substitutes. The caliper must produce a constant pressure of 10 grams per square millimeter throughout the range of skinfold thickness.

Scoring

The sum of the medians at each site is recorded as the student's score.

Sit-and-Reach

Rationale

Lower back pain continues to be a health problem of enormous magnitude. Measuring the distance a person can sit-and-reach is important in determining the functioning of the lower back and posterior thigh region.

Purpose

The purpose of the sit-and-reach is to measure the flexibility of the lower back and posterior thigh.

Instructions

The child assumes a sitting position with legs extended, feet shoulder width apart, and shoes off. The arms are extended forward with the hands one on top of the other with finger tips on top of fingernails. The child reaches directly forward, palms down on the surface of the scale four times, holding the position of maximum reach the last time for one full second. The legs must remain straight throughout the entire trial (Figure 2-5). Only one trial is given.

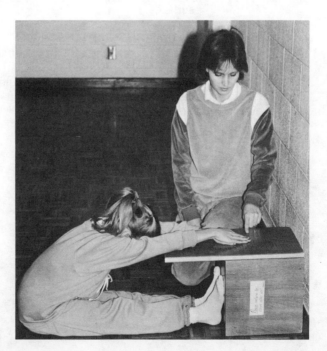

Figure 2-5 Sit and Reach Test for Flexibility

Organizational Hints

(1) Care should be taken to provide youngsters with adequate warm-up and stretch time prior to taking the test. (2) The trial should be considered invalid and readministered if the knees fail to remain fully extended throughout the fourth reach. (3) Without applying resistance, the instructor may place one hand on the student's knees to ensure that knees stay extended.

Test Area

Any area free of distractions is suitable for the administration of the sit-and-reach test.

Equipment and Supplies

A special apparatus consisting of a box with a measuring scale where 23 centimeters is at the level of the feet is required for this test.

Scoring

The score is the most distant point reached measured to the nearest centimeter.

Modified Sit-ups

Rationale

The number of successfully completed sit-ups is a good indicator of abdominal strength and endurance as well as functioning of the lower back.

Purpose

The purpose of the sit-up is to measure abdominal muscular strength and endurance.

Instructions

The child is positioned in a supine position with the legs bent at the knees, feet flat on the floor, and the heels between 12 to 18 inches from the buttocks (Figure 2–6a). Arms should be folded across the chest with hands on opposite shoulders. The forearms must remain in contact with the chest throughout the complete curl. The head is tucked with the chin to the chest. A partner holds the feet on the floor and counts the number of correctly executed sit-ups. The child curls to a sitting position until the elbows touch the thigh (Figure 2–6b). A successful sit-up is completed when the midback makes contact with the testing surface.

Organizational Hints

(1) Mats or individual carpet squares are recommended for comfort. (2) The modified sit-up should be regularly included in youngsters' planned physical activity. (3) The feet should be held by a partner to keep them in touch with the testing surface. (4) Rest between sit-ups is allowed in either the up or down position.

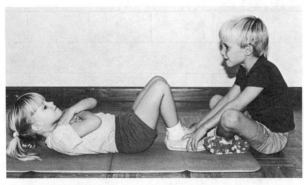

Figure 2–6(a)

Figure 2–6(b)

Test Area
Any area free of distractions is suitable for administering the timed sit-up test.

Equipment and Supplies
Stopwatch or watch with sweep hand and mats.

Scoring
The total number of correctly executed sit-ups in 1 minute is the score.

Pull-Ups

Rationale
Arm and shoulder girdle strength is important for the performance of so many health-related activities. Regular assessment of the capability of this particular group of muscles is important. The number of successfully completed pull-ups is a good indicator of upper arm and shoulder girdle strength and endurance.

Purpose
To measure general muscle strength and endurance.

Instructions
The student begins by hanging from a horizontal bar using an overhand grip (palms facing away). The arms should be fully extended with legs straight and together (Figure 2–7a). Feet should not be in contact with the floor. From this position, the student is instructed to raise the body (using only the arms) until the chin is positioned over the bar (Figure 2–7b). The student then returns to the starting position.

Organizational Hints
(1) The instructor should be positioned to prevent the student's legs from swinging during the pull-up phase. (2) A mat should be placed under the pull-up bar.

Figure 2-7(a)   **Figure 2-7(b)**

Test Area
A doorway, a small area for an inclined ladder, or a separate horizontal bar unit.

Equipment and Supplies
Metal or wooden bar approximately 1 1/2 inches diameter, a doorway gym bar, a piece of pipe, or an inclined ladder.

Scoring
The number of successfully completed pull-ups is recorded as the student's score.

HEALTH FITNESS STANDARDS The establishment of health fitness standards by the American Alliance for Health, Physical Education, Recreation, and Dance is based on the principle that the educational system should send children and youth into adulthood with a physical fitness status that provides a "buffer to the degeneration that inevitably comes with middle age" (AAHPERD, 1988). The standards printed in Figures 2–8 and 2–9 represent criteria that should serve as goals for youth to achieve.

OTHER TEST BATTERIES TO MEASURE HEALTH FITNESS Several other tests can be used to effectively measure and evaluate health-related physical fitness of children. The endorsing agency, itemized list of test components, and address for further information can be found in Table 2–4.

Using Student Self-Testing

One of the primary challenges of fitness development is to assist children in acquiring the necessary skills to solve their own fitness problems. To accomplish this, students need to acquire an understanding of the how and why of fitness and be able to assess and evaluate their personal level of physical fitness. While formal test batteries are useful for periodically assessing performance, introduc-

| Age | Test Item | | | | | |
	One Mile Walk/Run (minutes)	Sum of Skinfolds (mm)	Body Mass Index	Sit & Reach (cm)	Sit-up	Pull-up
5	14:00	16-36	14-20	25	20	1
6	13:00	16-36	14-20	25	20	1
7	12:00	16-36	14-20	25	24	1
8	11:30	16-36	14-20	25	26	1
9	11:00	16-36	14-20	25	28	1
10	11:00	16-36	14-21	25	30	1
11	11:00	16-36	14-21	25	33	1
12	11:00	16-36	15-22	25	33	1
13	10:30	16-36	15-23	25	33	1
14	10:30	16-36	17-24	25	35	1
15	10:30	16-36	17-24	25	35	1
16	10:30	16-36	17-24	25	35	1
17	10:30	16-36	17-25	25	35	1
18	10:30	16-36	18-26	25	35	1

Figure 2-8 Health Fitness Standards for Girls

Age	Test Item					
	One Mile Walk/Run (minutes)	Sum of Skinfolds (mm)	Body Mass Index	Sit & Reach (cm)	Sit-up	Pull-up
5	13:00	12-25	13-20	25	20	1
6	12:00	12-25	13-20	25	20	1
7	11:00	12-25	13-20	25	24	1
8	10:00	12-25	14-20	25	26	1
9	10:00	12-25	14-20	25	30	1
10	9:30	12-25	14-20	25	34	1
11	9:00	12-25	15-21	25	36	2
12	9:00	12-25	15-22	25	38	2
13	8:00	12-25	16-23	25	40	3
14	7:45	12-25	16-24	25	40	4
15	7:30	12-25	17-24	25	42	5
16	7:30	12-25	18-24	25	44	5
17	7:30	12-25	18-25	25	44	5
18	7:30	12-25	18-26	25	44	5

Figure 2-9 Health Fitness Standards for Boys

ing self-testing activities arms the student with the knowledge necessary to conduct fitness assessment, evaluation, and prescription during nonschool times.

Selection of self-testing activities should be based on several criteria. First, self-tests should measure components of fitness that are perceived important to the individual. Valuable fitness factors should be discussed in class prior to self-testing activities. Components that affect the child's physical health and well-being fall into this category.

Second, raw scores achieved from self-tests should be understandable and readily translatable into meaningful information. Children need immediate feedback regarding their performance. Scoring procedures that are easily understood and quickly converted into percentile equivalents via readable tables or microcomputer software are recommended.

Third, self-testing activities should have the potential to be conducted outside the physical education classroom with minimal amounts of instruments or inconvenience. Children should be encouraged to complete self-appraisals in a variety of settings outside school.

Following are examples of suggested self-testing activities.

CARDIOVASCULAR FITNESS

Kasch Pulse Recovery Test

Purpose
To determine heart rate recovery.

Equipment
A 12-inch high bench and a watch or clock with a second hand.

Instructions
Step on and off the bench at a rate of 24 steps per minute for 3 minutes. Sit down and relax for 5 seconds. Then take your pulse rate at either the wrist or carotid artery for 60 seconds and record it. Refer to Table 2-5 to evaluate the level of heart rate recovery.

Table 2-4 Additional Physical Fitness Testing and Awards Programs

Program	Item	Component Measured
FYT — Fit Youth Today American Health & Fitness Foundation 6225 U.S. Highway 290 East Suite 114 Austin TX 78723	Steady-state jog	Cardiorespiratory fitness
	Bent knee curl-up	Abdominal strength and endurance
	Sit and reach	Flexibility of lower back and posterior thigh
	Body composition	Body fat
FITNESSGRAM Institute for Aerobics Research 12330 Preston Road Dallas TX 75230	Mile run/walk	Cardiorespiratory fitness
	Body composition or BMI	Body fat
	Sit and reach	Flexibility of lower back and posterior thigh
	Sit-ups	Abdominal strength and endurance
	Pull-ups	Arm and shoulder strength and endurance
The Presidential Physical Fitness Award Program Department of Health and Human Services President's Council on Physical Fitness and Sports Washington DC 20001	Mile run/walk	Cardiorespiratory fitness
	V-sit reach or sit and reach	Flexibility of lower back and posterior thigh
	Curl-ups	Abdominal strength and endurance
	Pull-ups	Arm and shoulder strength and endurance
	Shuttle run	Agility and leg power

Mile Run

Purpose
To measure cardiovascular fitness.

Equipment
Any area that is flat, free from debris, and accurately measured. A watch or clock that measures minutes and seconds.

Instructions
See discussion on page 27.
Figures 2–8 and 2–9 provide age-group standards.

Table 2-5 Pulse Rate Table for 6–12 year olds

Fitness Levels	Boys	Girls
Excellent	73–82	81–92
Good	83–92	93–104
Average	93–103	105–118
Fair	104–113	119–130
Poor	114–123	131–142

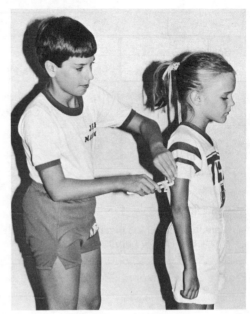

Figure 2–10 Self-Testing Body Composition

BODY COMPOSITION

Skinfold Test

Purpose
To determine percentage of body fat.

Equipment
Skinfold caliper. An effective homework assignment might be to have students determine their body composition (Figure 2–10).

Instructions
Follow directions as found in the *Physical Best* test manual.

A SUGGESTED SELF-TESTING APPROACH

One of the easiest ways to teach students the process of self-testing is to allow them an opportunity to work with a friend for the purpose of testing and recording scores. Allow students to pick a friend whom they feel comfortable with in physical performance activities. This both reduces personal embarrassment and the inclination to record false scores.

Four or five times a year, give students their self-testing cards and allow them to test themselves. Figure 2–11 is an example of a card that can be used for recording scores on the AAHPERD *Physical Best* fitness test. Note that a disclaimer is added so that, when parents review the card, they will understand that the results have been gathered by the youngsters and are not official results. Charts can be posted that convert the raw scores to percentiles so students can see how their scores compare with those of other students.

It is possible to organize the self-testing day so that students can perform sit-ups, skinfold measurements, and the sit-and-reach tests at one sitting. The mile run can then be done as a group test where students can record their own times by watching a large timing clock. The strength of this approach is that students learn to take skinfolds, measure the various components of fitness, and interpret the results. The scores gathered should be of concern only to the individual student and parents and should not be used for comparative purposes among students.

	Trial 1	Trial 2	Trial 3	Trial 4
Name_____Grade_____Room#_____Age _____				
School_____School ID #_____				
	Date_____	Date_____	Date_____	Date_____
	Score	Score	Score	Score
Distance Run (1 Mile)	_____	_____	_____	_____
Skinfold (mm)	_____	_____	_____	_____
Sit-Ups (In 60 sec.)	_____	_____	_____	_____
Sit/Reach	_____	_____	_____	_____
Pull-Ups	_____	_____	_____	_____

*Parents: Please note that results are not official scores.
This is a self-testing program in which students evaluate each other.

Figure 2–11 Personal Record Sheet—Physical Best Fitness Test*

Reporting Test Results to Parents

Physical fitness testing can serve as a good public relations tool for physical education. Elementary physical education has a unique opportunity to capitalize on the current high level of public awareness regarding the value of physical fitness. And nowhere can physical education gain a stronger base of support than with parents. Keeping parents informed about physical fitness testing is critical to the success of any program. Suggested strategies to apprise parents of ongoing fitness testing activities include educating, involving, and reporting.

Presenting the rationale for physical fitness and related activities is the initial step in educating parents about fitness testing. An excellent method for educating parents is through their children. Youngsters who are knowledgeable and fluent about physical fitness are likely to be the best campaigners for a quality physical education program. A planned evening demonstration is another opportunity to tell parents about the importance of physical fitness as well as reveal how physical fitness is being incorporated into physical education. Periodical physical education newsletters and/or personal letters discussing topics about physical fitness are also useful mechanisms to inform parents about fitness testing results.

Any fitness testing usually requires a great deal of the teacher's time and effort. Finding competent individuals to assist in the various phases of testing is not always easy. Involving interested parents with the administration of fitness testing may be an effective alternative to professional assistance. More importantly, becoming familiar with fitness testing through firsthand involvement answers many questions parents may have about the physical capabilities of their children. For example, to many parents, the thought of their child running a mile is alarming. Witnessing children successfully complete a mile run without stopping may cause parents to view the distance run test much more positively.

All testing procedures should include a follow-up report to parents. The report should include an explanation of test items, raw scores, percentile equivalents (with an explanation of how to interpret percentiles), and prescriptive activities to enhance fitness deficiencies.

The microcomputer is rapidly becoming a popular tool for assisting the practitioner in the recording and reporting of physical fitness scores (Figure 2–12). A payoff for using computer-assisted fitness testing is that the final report is usually personalized, easy to interpret, and meaningful to parents. Figure 2–13 shows a screen from the Health-Related Physical Fitness Student Profile program

Figure 2-12 Students Generating a Personalized Fitness Profile

HEALTH FITNESS PROFILE

Jacob				AGE:7
	MILE RUN	SKIN FOLD	SIT UPS	SIT & REACH
TERRIFIC !	☺			
GETTING THERE!!		☺		
WORK HARDER!			😐	
NEED LOTS OF WORK				☹
TEST SCORE	7:35	11.0	20	18
PERCENTILE	95	61	25	6

Figure 2-13 Computer-Generated Health Fitness Profile

Source: From D.N. Hastad and S.A. Plowman, The Health Fitness Profile for Children Ages 6–12. Hastings, Minnesota: CompTech Systems Design, 1985.

(Hastad & Plowman, 1985) which illustrates how fitness test results can be shown graphically by a computer. Ideal for keeping parents informed about their youngster's fitness, this program was written to be used by students. Students enter the results of their test items. Once the data are entered, students receive a personal fitness prescription in an animated fashion. The program automatically compares raw scores with national norms and offers a printed exercise prescription. This program is available from CompTech Systems Design. This company distributes a wide range of educational computer programs that are appropriate for use in the elementary school. Information and a catalog may be obtained from CompTech Systems Design, P.O. Box 516, Hastings MN 55033. AAHPERD Publications also offers a variety of microcomputer software packages that can assist in the collection and reporting of fitness scores. Additional software programs for elementary school physical education are described in *Dynamic Physical Education for Elementary School Children* (Dauer & Pangrazi, 1989) and *Measurement and Evaluation in Contemporary Physical Education* (Hastad & Lacy, 1989).

Promoting Physical Fitness

The elementary physical education curriculum should be designed to motivate all children to engage in physical activity in a manner that promotes fitness development. The physical education program can provide strong motivation for youngsters to achieve and maintain fitness. Some recommendations for promoting fitness follow:

1. An awards system that recognizes students who progress toward and achieve optimal health-related physical fitness should be established. Most of the current national test batteries include an award structure as part of their overall program.

2. Awards should be given for participation as well as achievement. If all children can achieve awards through effort, they will be motivated.

3. Bulletin boards that highlight physical fitness should be centrally displayed. Content of these boards should be kept up to date and should publicize the latest information about physical fitness.

4. Class time should be devoted to explaining the how and why of fitness. If children understand the rationale for active participation in vigorous sustained fitness routines, they are more apt to partake in an enthusiastic manner.

5. Self-testing should be an ongoing feature of the program. Children should have regular opportunities in the program to assess their fitness without concern about what others think.

6. Developing a positive relationship with parents is essential to the success of any fitness program. Fitness homework that must be signed off after completion by parents alerts adults about the importance of regular activity. A regularly published newsletter highlighting the importance of fitness is another way of making parents more aware of the ongoing efforts in physical education.

7. Supplemental programs such as intramurals, play days, recreational activities, special clubs, and so on should include an element of physical fitness. Playgrounds should also include apparatus that develops various components of physical fitness.

8. Fitness fairs and other exhibitions should be included as part of the public relations campaign for physical education. Evening and weekend activities can be conducted at schools, shopping malls, or other popular community locations.

References

AAHPERD. (1988). *Physical Best: The American Alliance Physical Fitness Education and Assessment Program.* Reston VA: Author.

Dauer, V. P., & Pangrazi, R. P. (1989). *Dynamic Physical Education for Elementary School Children.* New York: Macmillan.

Hastad, D. N., & Lacy, A. C. (1989). *Measurement and Evaluation in Contemporary Physical Education.* Scottsdale AZ: Gorsuch-Scarisbrick Publishers.

Hastad, D. N., & Plowman, S. A. (1985). *The Health Fitness Profile for Children* (software). Hastings MN: CompTech Systems Design.

Ross, J. G., & Gilbert, G. G. (1985). The National Council on Youth fitness study: A summary of the findings. *Journal of Physical Education, Recreation, and Dance, 56*(1), 45–50.

Suggested Supplementary References

AAHPERD. (1984). *Technical Manual: Health Related Physical Fitness.* Reston VA: Author.

Corbin, C. B., & Lindsey, R. (1988). *Concepts of Physical Fitness with Laboratories* (6th ed.). Dubuque IA: Wm. C. Brown.

Dotson, C. (1988). Health fitness standards. *Journal of Physical Education, Recreation, and Dance, 58*(7), 26–31.

Fox, K. R., & Biddle, S. J. (1988). The use of fitness tests: educational and psychological considerations. *Journal of Physical Education, Recreation, and Dance, 58*(2), 47–53.

Going, S. (1988). Physical Best: body composition in the assessment of youth fitness. *Journal of Physical Education, Recreation, and Dance, 58*(7), 32–36.

Kopperud, K. (1986). An emphasis on physical fitness. *Journal of Physical Education, Recreation, and Dance, 56*(7), 18–22.

Kuntzleman, C. T. (1977). *Heartbeat.* Spring Arbor MI: Arbor Press.

Kuntzleman, C. T. (1978). *Fitness Discovery Activities.* Spring Arbor MI: Arbor Press.

Liemohn, W. (1988). Flexibility and muscular strength. *Journal of Physical Education, Recreation, and Dance, 58*(7), 37–40.

Plowman, S. A., & Falls, H. B. (1978). AAHPER youth fitness test revision. *Journal of Physical Education and Recreation, 49*(9), 22–24.

CHAPTER THREE

Fitness for Special Populations

*F*itness is important for everyone. One of the problems one becomes aware of is the many exceptions that must be made for youngsters with special problems. Problems encountered in physical education that cause the most concern are obesity, asthma, mental retardation, and physical handicaps. Fitness has often been seen as the domain of the athletic and gifted. Fortunately, the belief that fitness is a need and right of all people is becoming more widespread. Methods and procedures for adapting the fitness activities found in Chapter 5 will constitute the focus of this discussion.

Obese Children

Obesity affects 30 to 50% of the American population depending on how this health problem is defined. Due to the magnitude of the problem, it is probably the most severe handicap facing children. One of the unfortunate myths associated with obesity is that youngsters will grow out of the condition when they enter adolescence. Sadly, this doesn't occur. What does happen is that children grow more deeply into obesity to a point where the problem becomes almost impossible to rectify. A case in point is that 28 of 29 teenagers who are obese will become obese adults (Johnson, 1956).

The typical triangle of treatment for obese children has been counseling, diet control, and exercise. It is difficult to find the opportunity for counseling in most elementary schools, and diet control is really not possible unless the parents' diet can be controlled. This leaves exercise and increased activity as the major area of focus in the treatment of obesity. Many studies have demonstrated that inactivity is the key factor in obesity. Bullen, Reed, and Mayer (1964) filmed adolescent girls participating in camp activities consisting of swimming, tennis, and volleyball. One group of girls was normal weight and a second group obese. The films were later analyzed to measure the amount of activity each group demonstrated. Activity was classified as anything but lying, standing, or sitting. When the two groups were compared, it was found that the obese group was two and a half times less active in swimming and tennis, and one and one half times less active in volleyball as compared to the nonobese group. The researchers concluded that inactivity is a significant factor in perpetuating obesity.

Corbin and Fletcher (1968) conducted a similar study in which they analyzed diet and activity patterns of obese and nonobese elementary school boys and girls. Their results were similar to those of Bullen, et al. (1964), and they concluded that "inactivity may be as important or more important than excessive caloric intake in the development and maintenance of childhood obesity." A related finding was that diets were similar among all children regardless of body fat proportions.

Many people do not consider exercise to be a serious factor in weight control since they know that running a mile will only burn 80 to 110 calories. Since they are aware that it is necessary to burn approximately 3500 calories to lose a pound of weight, they assume that it is impossible to lose weight in this manner. It is important to look at the long-term effect of exercise to understand how important it can be in weight control. Assume a student is encouraged to walk a mile each day and burns off 100 calories per mile. Over a period of 35 days, if all other factors remain equal, a total of 3500 extra calories will be metabolized. This will result in a net loss of 1 pound of weight. If this regimen is maintained for a year, the amount of weight lost will be 10 pounds. Obviously, this dramatic weight loss is the result of only an increase of daily activity. The point to remember is that the additive effect of exercise can be quite dramatic and convincing.

Another advantage to using aerobic type activities for obese children is that they have an impact on caloric expenditure. Sharkey (1978) reported that approximately 30 minutes of vigorous and demanding activity will not only burn more calories during exercise, but will double caloric expenditure for 6 hours following the exercise period. Based on the discussion above, the program described here will focus on increasing the obese child's activity level.

When dealing with obese children, it is important to remember that scale weight is usually not an effective evaluation tool. When working with preadolescent youngsters, many teachers have made the assumption that if scale weight can be maintained or lost, the program will be successful. We have found this to be an unreasonable goal. Over an 18-week period, youngsters have consistently gained an average of 3 to 5 pounds of weight and grown 1 inch or more in height. However, at the same time, their skinfold measurements have decreased an average 1 to 2 millimeters. What this demonstrates is that it is impossible for growing youngsters to maintain or lose weight. They can, however, gain weight while losing body fat. It also reinforces the importance of skinfold measurements as described in the *Physical Best: Fitness Education and Assessment Program* (AAHPERD, 1988).

Teachers must understand that the obese youngster finds it difficult to participate in aerobic activity. It is not uncommon for a youngster with this problem to dislike physical activity. If you choose to help obese children, it is important to be gentle, concentrate on small increments of success, and to avoid failure. Nothing is more devastating to children who want to lose weight than to find out, after 18 weeks of activity, that they have been unsuccessful even though the teacher helped. Working with obese youngsters should hold no false pretense and should focus on personal effort and dedication. It also points out that working with the grossly obese youngster is probably in poor judgment. Seldom are physical education teachers successful in helping the highly obese. This type child is in need of medical help and should be referred to the school nurse.

IMPLEMENTING A PROGRAM FOR OBESE YOUNGSTERS

There are three key individuals responsible for developing a successful fitness program for obese children: the child, the teacher, and the parent(s). If one of the three is uninterested in dealing with the problem, then the odds are high that the program will not be successful. The child must realize there is a problem and want to solve it, the teacher must have a genuine concern for the child and want to help, and the parents must be willing to help at home. It is important to have a conference with both parents and child to assure they want to work cooperatively. An awareness of what to expect from parents is important since statistics show that obese children generally come from homes where parents are obese. Where both parents are obese, 80% of the children will be obese. If both parents are normal weight, only 8% of the youngsters will be obese. This dictates a sensitive approach to the problem since many of the parents may also be obese.

Selection of Program Participants

This is a critical step in that every effort should be made to include students who have a high probability for success. The *Physical Best: Fitness Assessment and Education Program* can be used to screen students for a minimal level of physical fitness. For example, we have had success with accepting students into the program if they are not extremely obese. Students well beyond the recommended criteria are usually too obese for treatment in a physical education setting. The better youngsters score on the mile run-walk test, the stronger the possibility that they will be willing to participate in aerobic activities. It should be added that emphasis should be placed on the walking aspect of this test since many of these youngsters will not be in adequate physical condition to run a mile.

Other data can be gathered to facilitate selection. Evaluative data is most helpful for taking an objective look at the youngster. It avoids the emotional approach to selection of students which can result in false hope. The data is also most helpful at a later stage in demonstrating clearly the progress (or lack there of) the student is making. Examples of further evaluation that can be done are height and weight, attitude inventories such as the *Children's Attitude Toward Physical Activity* (Simon & Smoll, 1974), and self-concept scales. It can be most encouraging to teachers and parents to see that the program has resulted in a more positive feeling toward physical activity. One final point in selecting students for inclusion: Some schools have had excellent success in establishing a fitness council. This group can include a classroom teacher, principal, school nurse, parent, and counselor. The bottom line is to select students who can be successfully treated in the program.

Parental Involvement

Few programs will be successful if parents do not stand fully behind them. The following points will help generate needed support:

1. A meeting should be held with parents of *potential* candidates. The purpose of the meeting is to see if they are genuinely interested in helping and supporting their youngster's efforts. Topics that should be covered in the meeting are objectives of the program, data that demonstrates and explains why their youngster has been classified as obese, and the responsibilities of both student and parent.

2. Parents should be given a handout that explains the program and related responsibilities of the parent and child. This allows both parties to discuss the program at home without outside pressure.

3. Parents should understand that the program will not continue if either the parent or child fails to uphold designated responsibilities.

4. A permission slip should be handed out at the meeting which both student and parent sign after the in-home discussion and return indicating whether or not they want to participate.

Implementing the Program

One of the first questions to answer is whether to group youngsters homogeneously or heterogeneously. One advantage of grouping obese youngsters in one class for exercise and activity is ease of administration for the teacher (but not for the school as a whole). To some degree, they have something in common and grouping may ease the embarrassment of the situation. On the other hand, the problems of obesity are varied and demand a great deal of individual attention. Grouping obese youngsters also creates an unreal environment that may cause both participants and teachers to lower their expectations due to the fact that there are no "normal" performers in the class. An approach that has been successful is to offer a one-on-one meeting with the teacher once a week. In the meeting, the teacher can discuss the student's progress, listen to problems the child is having, and offer direction and activity assignment for the student. The emphasis of this approach should be to increase the amount of activity the child participates in *independently of the class.* This approach meets the personal needs of each student and allows that activity to be adapted to those needs. It also is more in line with actual life styles in that students are responsible for performing the assigned activity without someone looking over their shoulder or pushing them. Many approaches to obesity have been successful as long as someone was monitoring the program. However, when students leave the program, the excessive weight problem recurs.

ASSIGNING ACTIVITY The following points can be used as guidelines in assigning increased aerobic activity for youngsters. The activity should be enjoyable and result in an increase in the amount of aerobic endurance activity accomplished by the child.

1. Activity assigned to the youngster should be aerobic in nature. The assignment should be *in addition* to the amount of activity the student normally participates in during a typical school day.

2. Prescription should be based on the child's tolerance for exercise. This means that it is important to understand the child's capabilities. If the exercise assignment is too easy, little will be gained. On the other hand, if the assignment is too difficult, the child may be turned off and discouraged by the program.

3. Record the activity assignment in order to assure that gradual overload and progression are occurring. The records can also be excellent motivators for the participant to demonstrate how much progress has occurred over the duration of the program.

4. Offer two or three aerobic activities the youngster enjoys. It is important to avoid boredom in the early stages of the program. Choices will also start to teach the child that there are different types of activity that can facilitate fitness development.

5. Assignments should be made in minutes per day. If the youngster is in poor physical condition, the assignments may have to be short bouts of activity done throughout the day. As fitness improves, the amount of continuous activity done at one time can be increased. A recommended starting point is 10 minutes of exercise daily. Increase the dosage by 2 minutes weekly until a maximum of 30 to 40 minutes is reached.

6. The following are examples of activities that may be enjoyable for the obese child: walking, skate-boarding, roller-skating, ice-skating, bicycling, moto-cross biking, hiking, unorganized "sandlot" games, orienteering, jogging, swimming, and rope jumping.

Any fitness program for the obese child must to be designed to accept the inherent limitations of the participants. Not only do obese youngsters find it more difficult to exercise, they also have little or no predisposition to exercise. Since there are so many obese youngsters in today's society, it becomes extremely important to deal with this malady.

The Asthmatic Child

Asthma is a disease of hyperreactive (very sensitive) airways that, from time to time, become obstructed, making movement of air more difficult. This disease is a complex problem that has challenged medical science for years. Chronic asthma is the number one cause of school absences in the United States. The impact of this disease on physical education participation is even more widespread.

Asthma attacks may be minor and short in duration with little discomfort, or severe and of long duration. Exercise in excess of 5 minutes is a trigger mechanism for symptoms in asthmatic children. The most common symptoms take the form of wheezing after exercising, or simply coughing. In many cases, affected children are not aware of the acute signs of asthma, but realize that they tire more easily than their friends. Despite this, asthmatic children should be encouraged to participate in vigorous and sustained physical activity. Being an asthmatic does not mean that an individual is unable to or prohibited from participating in exercise and sport. In fact, during the 1984 Olympics, 30 medals were awarded to asthmatic members of the U.S. Olympic team. Jackie Joyner-Kersee's recent Olympic gold medal efforts in the heptathalon and long jump were accomplished in spite of a long history of asthma. There are many other famous sports personalities and world-class athletes who are living examples of asthmatics who achieved success in sport.

Research findings have demonstrated that asthmatic children can benefit greatly from exercise. The physical fitness benefits (i.e., improved cardiovascular fitness, flexibility, and so on) derived from properly planned and delivered exercise programs are the same for asthmatics as for normal children. Through active participation in prolonged exercise, asthmatic children can also develop self-esteem and confidence. With mild symptoms or between the episodes of severe asthma, the youngsters may be at little or no disadvantage in most activities. Aerobic activities such as jogging, pace walking, aerobic dance, biking, continuous skate-boarding, swimming, and so on can become a part of an asthmatic's life style.

Asthmatic children need to develop and maintain a level of physical fitness that provides the strength, stamina, and degree of flexibility to learn important fundamental movement skills and lead a healthy life. If exercise is a trigger for their asthma, they need to learn to detect changes in their breathing patterns and inform the instructor if they are having trouble. If the wheezing persists, they should take a brief rest until it subsides, then continue participation in the activity.

Many times exercise-induced asthma can be blocked by proper medication taken prior to exercise. Most children who use medication for this purpose have become skillful users of the meter-dose inhalers and require little monitoring. Teachers should become familiar with the medication needs and dosage requirements of youngsters who use inhalers to block wheezing episodes. The best source of explanation for this situation would be the parents or a medical doctor.

Asthmatic children can do a great deal to help themselves gain relief from wheezing episodes. The physical education teacher can be instrumental in assisting and encouraging the children to practice these techniques regularly. Following are the most common steps for an asthmatic to follow in attempting to control a wheezing episode (Dennis, 1979):

1. At the onset of a wheeze, the child should sit down and rest. During an attack, the muscles of the airways contract making it difficult to breath. Relaxing the entire body assists in reducing the degree of unwanted muscular contraction. The most effective resting position would be sitting with the back straight and arms hanging down loosely at the sides.

2. Diaphragmatic breathing is accomplished when the diaphragm (area of the stomach) is moved downward and outward during inspiration and back during expiration. Depending on the severity of the attack, this technique should be practiced for at least several minutes.

3. If wheezing persists, have the youngster sit down and drink up to three cups of warm, clear liquid. Warm water is usually the most practical and commonly used.

If these three steps prove to be ineffective in stopping the wheezing, medication is likely warranted.

MEDICAL CONSIDERATIONS

The problems associated with asthma have a physiological basis and often surface during or after exercise. Many parents assume that their child will outgrow asthma. This is not the case. An individual with asthma will always be susceptible to an attack. Sometimes youngsters can live symptom-free for an extended length of time and, when they least expect it, an attack can be triggered. Many times this recurrence of asthma is the result of infection. In sum, asthma is not cured. Recent advances in medication and a better understanding of the disease make asthma much easier to control than has previously been the case.

The ways in which exercise can induce an asthmatic attack are quite predictable. Anaerobic activities consisting of exercises of short duration that do not require efficient use of oxygen by the body generally do not cause bronchoconstriction. On the other hand, aerobic activities that require the body to efficiently utilize oxygen over a sustained period can prompt wheezing. Distance running, cross-country skiing, aerobic dance, distance cycling, and other continuously sustained activities have been found to cause broncho-constriction. In the elementary physical education environment, the instructor should be able to monitor the breathing patterns of youngsters with asthma without difficulty. If wheezing commences, the children should be encouraged to slow down and begin a relaxed pattern of breathing.

There are several physical signs that are symptoms of an asthma attack:

1. A wheezing child will usually have a look of discomfort and distress. This "pained" appearance is quite distinctive and becomes more apparent with continued exercise.

2. The muscles of the shoulder girdle and neck are constricted. The child appears to be slumping forward.

3. Breathing becomes shallow and the rate of respiration is more rapid than normal.

4. A shrill, high pitched sound is often heard. This wheezing sound is caused by trapped air passing through the constricted airways.

"The effective care of the child during bronchoconstriction often depends on the instructor recognizing these symptoms, understanding the dynamics of bronchoconstriction operative in the student, estimating levels of respiratory distress, and responding appropriately" (Dennis, 1985, p. 5).

INVOLVING ASTHMATICS IN PHYSICAL EDUCATION

Children with asthma should be expected to be active participants in physical education class. Encouraging these youngsters to be involved in vigorous fitness routines will help develop a typically underdeveloped cardiorespiratory system and strengthen upper-body musculature. Through participation in aerobic activities, the teacher and child will develop an understanding of the activity level that provokes an asthma attack. Recognizing this point will provide the information needed to modify activities, indicate those activities that will not cause undue respiratory distress, and serve as a benchmark for setting personal fitness goals.

Physical education is important to the asthmatic child. Most asthmatic children can participate in vigorous physical activities with minimal difficulty, provided the asthma is under satisfactory control. All physical education activities should be encouraged but evaluated on an individual basis for each asthmatic child, depending on tolerance for duration and intensity of effort (Committee on Children with Disabilities and Committee on Sports Medicine, 1984).

Fitness for Handicapped Children

Fitness opportunities for handicapped children must be offered in the school setting. Federal law requires that school districts provide physical education services for all handicapped and/or disabled students. Many terms have been used by educators and the general public to describe persons who are handicapped. Impaired, disabled, special, and unique are among the words used to describe individuals with special needs. What is paramount is the fact that these individuals, regardless of their condition, are people and have the same fitness needs as their able-bodied peers. The fitness objectives do not necessarily change for these children; rather, the means to achieve health fitness goals may require modification.

This section is based on the practice of mainstreaming handicapped youngsters into the physical education class setting. It is beyond the scope of this text to offer a total fitness program developed specifically for handicapped children. Mainstreaming involves a compromise if the needs of all participants are going to be realized. However, the personal rewards and social learning the handicapped youngsters can gain certainly offset the inconvenience felt by many teachers involved in mainstreaming practices.

Mainstreaming is the practice of placing children with mental, emotional, or physical disabilities into classes with able youngsters. Placement of these children requires a cooperative effort among the principal, teacher, parents, and special education representative. These professionals must make sure that the mainstreaming places the child in a setting that ensures achievement and success. The youngster should feel comfortable in the environment and not detract from the learning of others in the class. There are many approaches used in the practice of mainstreaming; the most commonly used are as follows:

1. *Full mainstreaming.* Handicapped youngsters participate as full-time members of a physical education class. Within their limitations, they participate in physical education activities with nonhandicapped peers.

2. *Partial mainstreaming.* Students take part in selected physical education activities but do not meet on a full-time basis due to their inability to find success in some activities. Developmental needs that cannot be met in the regular physical education class are met in special classes.

3. *Reverse mainstreaming.* Nonhandicapped children are brought into a special physical education class to promote intergroup peer relationships.

Although mainstreaming is commonly used in the physical education setting, there are few valid guidelines available for the physical education specialist. The advantages of mainstreaming are no longer questioned. What is questioned is how to mainstream effectively. Many teachers have little or no training to deal with handicapped youngsters. The burden of responsibility falls on the teacher to retrain both in terms of attitude and instructional expertise. The handicapped youngsters must be seen as members of the class with the same privileges and needs as others.

A responsible decision needs to be made as to whether the handicapped child is capable of being mainstreamed. The child must be able to accomplish the large majority, if not all, of the activities being taught in the class. It is not fair to teacher or student to place a child into a setting where failure is predetermined. The program should focus on what the youngster can do rather than what he or she can't do. Any approach that treats the handicapped child as a cripple dehumanizes the youngster and the result is worse than no program at all.

All students in the class should find the opportunity to be challenged and make progress. The educational needs of the handicapped must be met without jeopardizing the progress of other students. This does not rule out some activity modifications so the handicapped can be included. Some adapted equipment might be necessary. A wonderful fact about fitness activity is that it demands little special equipment and uses low-level motor patterns which the majority of students are capable of performing.

INTEGRATING SPECIAL STUDENTS INTO PHYSICAL EDUCATION CLASSES

In the long run, the most important factor in teaching the handicapped child is the attitude and concern directed toward the child. Certainly, the teacher should be most concerned about enhancing physical fitness levels in all youngsters. However, if the atmosphere is not one of care and concern, any increase in the degree of physical fitness may be outweighed by the traumatic and emotionally scarring experience. Following are guidelines that may facilitate successful integration of the child into the physical education setting:

1. Involve other professionals and parents in helping the child find success. If it is important for the child to be mainstreamed into physical education, then an aide or teacher should make the transition a smooth one. If the teacher and student get off on the wrong foot, the experience may be very negative. Having support personnel available to help the mainstreamed child learn the exercises and routines will facilitate the experience for all concerned.

2. Instructional focus should be on the ability and strengths of the child. Strong attempts should be made to avoid situations that give rise to embarrassment such as performing in front of others, running laps while early finishers observe, and holding contests to see who is strongest, fastest, and so on.

3. Peer acceptance of the mainstreamed child is enhanced when students observe the instructor responding to the child in a warm, caring manner. In most cases, the instructor's *behavior* will speak louder than his or her *words*.

4. Focus should be on physical activities the youngster can perform. Ignore situations where the child's handicap prevents successful performance. Generate excitement and enthusiasm when performance improves so other students are aware of the progress being made.

5. Effective record keeping is important so that parents and classroom instructors are aware of progress. Progress is motivating to all parties concerned and should relate improvement in the various areas of fitness. Microcomputer software to assist the teacher in database management and developing individualized education programs is available from commercial vendors.

6. Teachers sometimes feel that they shouldn't have to modify instruction and programs to meet the needs of the special child. However, this sort of stubbornness will only serve to erode the child's confidence. All effective teachers constantly modify their approaches and techniques for all children, regardless of handicap.

7. If a special education consultant is available, he or she should be used for support and evaluative services. When the consultant observes and evaluates the fitness presentation, he or she may be able to offer insight and advice to make the instructional approach much more effective.

8. Using paraprofessionals or interns from local colleges or universities can provide valuable assistance in working with handicapped youngsters. These trained individuals can provide the individual attention often required by children with special needs.

When the guidelines are observed, it becomes clear that they primarily speak to sound instructional practices based on love, concern, and enthusiasm. Mainstreaming does create a more varied and challenging environment for the teacher. There is little question that it will take more work to assure success for all. However, if it doesn't occur, the chance for offering the special child a lifetime of fitness may be lost.

MODIFYING PARTICIPATION

As mentioned above, activities have to be modified in order to help the special child find success. Judgments have to be made based on the child's fitness level and type of impairment. Whenever possible, the situation should be modified so the youngster feels as though he or she has made a contribution to the total class. All children have a right to feel important and needed.

Following are some suggestions for modifying various situations in order to enhance effective participation:

1. A first step is to observe the youngster for the first few sessions. This will offer insight into how much the child is capable of performing. Try to develop a role in fitness activities that is based on the child's competency so the experience is as natural as possible.

2. Adapt rules to assure the child has a chance for success. Success shouldn't be guaranteed or the activity will not be challenging. For example, if running is the activity, the handicapped child may be given a different challenge than regular students. It may be effective to ask the child for feedback about what is challenging to him or her. Many children will want the task modified only slightly since they feel the need to be challenged, not pampered.

3. Progression and overload are extremely important variables that should be monitored closely with handicapped children. It may be necessary to vary the intensity and time factors (see Chapter 2) in order to assure that the handicapped youngster is not overfatigued.

4. Situations that help regular and handicapped students understand each other can be arranged. For example, a handicapped youngster in braces might exercise with a regular student performing on borrowed crutches. Regular students could be placed in wheelchairs to understand the tremendous effort needed to exercise in this setting. This technique can often generate empathy and understanding for all students involved.

5. If squads are to be used, make sure they are organized in a manner that is not degrading, for example, letting captains choose their friends until the handicapped or obese youngsters are the only people left.

6. If fitness games are being played, change the rules so no players are eliminated. Often, the players eliminated earliest are those who need the activity the most. If points are scored when a player is tagged, the point system can be varied so the handicapped youngster with limited mobility is penalized to a lesser degree.

7. Squads should be equalized and rotated on a regular basis so that special children are equally divided. Changing the membership of squads on a regular basis will allow youngsters to understand and communicate with children possessing varying handicaps.

8. Modify equipment and facilities as needed. Jogging tracks of varying distances and pull-up bars at different heights are examples of modifications based on the needs of participants.

9. Learn to teach using both verbal and visual hand signals. This will facilitate learning for students with hearing problems.

10. It may be necessary to have an aide or another student (cross-age tutoring by older students) teach the special child prior to the mainstreaming. This is sometimes necessary since handicapped youngsters are unwilling to try due to embarrassment and fear of failure. Confidence can be developed on a one-to-one basis or in small-group settings.

Physical fitness is important for handicapped children. As with able children, physical fitness attainment is a primary goal for the handicapped child. Achieving an appropriate level of fitness can improve the child's appearance, make routine moving from room to room less laborious, and generally enhance the self-confidence of the student.

The focus of all the techniques mentioned in this chapter should be to smoothly integrate the youngster into the class setting. Fitness activities and exercises mentioned in Chapter 5 can be used (and modified as needed) with handicapped children. The more often special children can be made to feel like "real" and important members of the class, the more chance there is for progress. The ability of special children should not be underestimated. Expect them to perform and improve their personal fitness levels.

References

AAHPERD. (1988). *Physical Best: The American Alliance Physical Fitness Assessment and Education Program.* Reston VA: Author.

Bullen, B., Reed, R., Mayer, J. (1964). Physical activity of obese and nonobese adolescent girls appraised by motion picture sampling. *American Journal of Clinical Nutrition, 14,* 211–223.

Committee on Children with Disabilities and Committee on Sports Medicine. (1984). The asthmatic child's participation in sports and physical education. *Pediatrics, 74*(1), 155–156.

Corbin, C. B., & Fletcher, P. (1968). Diet and physical activity patterns of obese and nonobese elementary school children. *Research Quarterly, 39*(4), 922–928.

Dennis, W. (1985). *What Every Physical Educator Should Know About Asthma.* Denver CO: National Jewish Hospital and Research Center.

Johnson, M. L. (1956). The prevalence and incidence of obesity in a cross section of elementary and secondary school children. *American Journal of Clinical Nutrition, 4,* 37.

Sharkey, B. (1978). *Physiological Fitness and Weight Control.* Missoula MT: Mountain Press.

Simon, J., & Smoll, F. (1974). An instrument for assessing children's attitudes toward physical activity. *Research Quarterly, 45*(4), 407–415.

Representative Readings

Adams, R. C., et al. (1982). *Games, Sports and Exercises for the Physically Handicapped* (3rd. ed.). Philadelphia: Lea & Febiger.

Bishop, P. (1988). *Adapted Physical Education: A Comprehensive Resource Manual of Definition Assessment, Programming and Future Predictions.* Kearney NE: Educational Systems Associated, Inc., P.O. Box 96, Kearney NE 68847.

Bundschugh, E. *Project Dart Physical Education for Handicapped Students.* Northbrook IL: Hubbard, P.O. Box 104, Northbrook IL 60062.

Hirst, C. C., & Michaelis, E. *Retarded Kids Need to Play.* New York: Leisure Press, 597 Fifth Ave., New York NY 10017.

Jones, J. A. *Training Guide to Cerebral Palsy Sports* (3rd ed.). Champaign IL: Human Kinetics Books, Box 5076, Champaign IL 61820.

National Jewish Center for Immunology and Respiratory Medicine. (1986). *Your Child and Asthma.* Denver CO: Author.

National Jewish Center for Immunology and Respiratory Medicine. (1985). *Asthma.* Denver CO: Author.

Ohio Department of Education. *Implementing Effective Physical Education for Handicapped Children* and *Improving Physical Education for the Handicapped in Ohio.* Columbus: Ohio Department of Education, Division of Elementary and Secondary Education, 65 South Front Street, Columbus OH 43215.

Stein, Julian U., consultant. (1972). *Special Olympics Instructional Manual.* Washington DC: AAHPER & The Joseph P. Kennedy, Jr. Foundation. (AAHPER, 1201 Sixteenth Street, N.W., Washington, D.C. 20036. The Joseph P. Kennedy, Jr. Foundation, 1701 K Street, N.W., Washington, D.C. 20006.)

Vodola, T. M. *Diagnostic-Prescriptive Motor Ability and Physical Fitness Tasks and Activities for the Normal and Atypical Individual.* Bloomfield NJ: C.F. Wood Company, Inc.

Walsh, H., & Holland, T. (1984). *Get Fit.* Alberta, Canada: The University of Alberta. Research and Training Centre for the Physically Disabled, Department of Physical Education and Sport Studies, The University of Alberta, Edmonton, Alberta, Canada.

CHAPTER FOUR

Knowledge and Attitudes for Lifetime Fitness

*I*mproving the physical fitness of children is an essential outcome of elementary physical education. Successful attainment of acceptable levels of physical fitness is almost entirely dependent on the physical education delivery system. Teacher behavior, types of activity, time allotment, length of class period, and other factors variously influence the degree to which the physical fitness objective can be met. It is well known that the fitness of children can be developed and maintained through carefully monitored assessment and evaluation techniques and a balanced systematic approach to the presentation of fitness routines. But, if physical fitness is to be a lifetime pursuit, youngsters must develop a cognition about the how and why of fitness and positive attitudes toward vigorous physical activity and exercise. What we must understand is that realizing immediate fitness expectations through regimented calisthenics is only a short-term solution to a long-term problem.

Results of recent research investigations are dispelling the myth that children freely participate in physical activity with sufficient FIT to incur a training effect. It should come as no surprise that a child's inclination toward only moderate physical activity during free play time, with less than acceptable degrees of FIT, has been repeatedly verified through observational studies designed to establish movement frequency during periods of recess and recreation (Cumming, 1975; Hovell, Bursick, Sharkey, & McClure, 1978). The health-related physical fitness of children also has been found to deteriorate during the months of summer vacation (Hastad & Pangrazi, 1983). Mounting evidence suggests that children do not appear to have a "biological handicap" in performing prolonged sessions of exercise, but rather, seldom engage in extended physical activity because they perceive it to be monotonous (Macek & Vavra, 1974).

In an attempt to offset children's apparent disinterest in vigorous physical activity during free time and to encourage participation in fitness-related activities, it becomes imperative to implement strategies designed to develop cognition about and positive attitudes toward physical fitness. If we accept the premise that understanding and appreciating physical activity and the self are prerequisites to voluntary participation in fitness-related activities, then we must also be sure that children enjoy physical activity and acquire the necessary cognitive skills to make sensible and knowledgeable decisions about personal physical activity habits.

Developing Positive Attitudes Toward Fitness

Exercise can contribute to improved physical well-being and enhanced quality of life for individuals of all ages. Developing a positive attitude about physical activity should begin during the formative years. Initially, emphasis should be placed on enjoying the activity and better understanding the body's capacity for physical performance. Since children can exercise regularly and are physiologically well equipped for endurance activity and perform well in aerobic exercise, fitness routines that promote enjoyment of vigorous exercise should be presented. The following instructional strategies can be used to make exercise more enjoyable for children:

1. Instructors should individualize exercise to accommodate the various stages of physical growth and development demonstrated by elementary school children. Students who are expected to participate in fitness activities but, due to delayed physical maturity, find themselves unable to perform some or all exercises are not likely to develop a positive attitude toward physical activity.

2. Children should be exposed to a wide variety of physical fitness routines and exercises. Presenting diverse fitness opportunities not only decreases the monotony of doing the same routines week after week, it also increases the likelihood that the children will experience activities that are personally enjoyable. Avoiding potential boredom by systematically changing the type of and approach to fitness activities is a significant step in helping children perceive fitness as being something positive.

3. Youngsters should acquire an understanding about physical fitness. Developing a cognition about the value of being physically fit, how to apply the principles of exercise, and how fitness can become part of one's life style can positively alter children's outlook toward physical activity. Planned minilessons that present the various concepts of fitness or simply calling the class together at the end of the lesson to discuss key fitness points learned during class can assist in promoting a clearer understanding of why fitness is important.

4. Children should be assured of success in fitness activities. Everyone enjoys success, especially children. Youngsters become motivated to perform when they sense that success is possible. Planning fitness activities so that all children can succeed is not a simple task. Teachers must have a working knowledge of the physical performance capabilities and limitations of each child and set goals accordingly. Expectations must be realistic and attainable. Realization of fitness goals can only serve to foster a positive outlook toward physical activity.

5. Teacher feedback in the form of verbal/nonverbal behavior or written comments can also contribute to the way children view fitness activities. Immediate, accurate, and specific feedback regarding performance encourages continued participation. Provided in a positive manner, this feedback can stimulate children to extend participation in exercise beyond the confines of the gymnasium.

6. Role modeling is another device that can influence children's attitudes toward physical fitness. We must remember that a teacher, through appearance, attitude, and actions, exemplifies an "end product." Teachers who continually express a physical vitality, take pride in being active, participate in fitness activities with the children, and are physically fit clearly are able to positively influence children's attitudes about an active life style.

Decision Making for Fitness

While disappointing, the progressive decline in children's physical fitness and the renewed national emphasis on health, physical well-being, and an active life style can be viewed as positive events for physical education. With the public eye focused directly on student outcomes, physical education has the unique opportunity to establish itself as an indispensable component of a child's educational experience.

The school's first responsibility is to provide opportunities for the youngsters to achieve the goal of developing and maintaining a level of physical fitness commensurate with their needs. This responsibility can be fulfilled through a systematic and balanced approach to physical fitness. The school's responsibility, however, does not end with improved scores. Children must be provided with the information necessary to translate what the teacher tells them to do into doing things on their own. Youngsters must begin to establish their own exercise patterns and learn how to self-test and interpret the results. Most importantly, they must begin learning how to plan and be responsible for a personal exercise program. Steps must be taken to assure that children are given opportunities to acquire the skills necessary for making thoughtful decisions about their fitness program. Suggested tactics to facilitate acquisition of decision-making skills include:

1. *Involving the children in the development of purposeful and realistic goals.* Fitness goals that are viewed as worthwhile and attainable and that have been determined, at least in part, by the children are more likely to prompt child-initiated activity than goals established solely by the teacher.

2. *Providing personalized learning opportunities.* Intermediate-grade students can benefit from learning activities that might include self-testing, assisting in administration and scoring of fitness tests, and interpreting health fitness items.

3. *Relying on self-discovery techniques.* Through self-discovery activities and various teaching styles, teachers can create learning situations that place children in decision-making positions.

4. *Encouraging participation in out-of-school fitness activities.* Rewarding the exercise patterns of youngsters during nonschool time can assist in motivating them to self-select into vigorous physical activity.

5. *Allowing students to select the fitness activities.* Providing alternative exercises encourages children to make personal choices.

Leading Discussions on Wellness

Physical fitness refers to the general overall physical health and well-being of an individual. *Wellness*, on the other hand, means more than "feeling good." It refers to attainment of a special type of life style and focuses on living life to the fullest.

The popularity of wellness programs is apparent. Major medical centers, colleges and universities, business corporations, and even high schools are implementing programs that emphasize personal wellness planning. It is ironic that planned efforts in wellness education have only recently filtered down into the elementary schools.

The primary goal of a wellness program in the elementary school is to establish a fundamental basis for effective living. Wellness instruction in the elementary school should be a shared responsibility. Some aspects of wellness, such as development of a personalized level of physical fitness, are the responsibility of the physical educator. Many other topics, such as substance abuse, stress, obesity, and nutrition, can be included in science and health units taught by the classroom teacher with added support from the physical education teacher.

Movement is the basis for physical education. We do not recommend substituting a knowledge-based discussion for physical activity. However, activity without a rudimentary knowledge about how and why may limit the desired long-term fitness benefits. If wellness topics cannot be incorporated into the schoolwide curricula, then it becomes the responsibility of the physical educator to devise a means for providing wellness instruction to the students. Effective alternative approaches to teaching wellness concepts in physical education are:

1. *The minilesson.* This is a brief (no more than 5 minutes) instructional episode focusing on a particular aspect of wellness.

2. *Block scheduling.* Several nonconsecutive weeks during the school year are dedicated to the teaching of wellness concepts. While this means canceling physical education, the resulting concentrated instruction in an uninterrupted classroom setting is conducive to cognitive and affective learning.

Leading discussions on wellness topics require the teacher to effectively establish and maintain a climate conducive to open communication. The following teacher behaviors are necessary for successful discussions:

Structuring is used to help the teacher create a situation that facilitates unrestricted communication.

Focus setting is used to clearly identify the topic of discussion.

Clarifying is used to illicit a better understanding of the students' comments.

Acknowledging is used to communicate to the students that spoken comments have been understood and useful to the discussion.

Teacher silence indicates to the students that it is their responsibility to carry on the discussion.

Wellness Topics for Discussion

It is important to remember that the basis for physical education is movement. Teachers must be careful not to devote excessive amounts of physical education time to discussions. Instead, wellness discussions should be judiciously planned to coincide with functional rest periods interspersed throughout the lesson or reserved for the end of the class. To maintain the students' interest, topics should be timely, pertinent, and understandable. When presenting topics it is important to highlight key concepts associated with the topic and to provide selected learning experiences that may assist children in better understanding the concept. Suggested wellness topics are exercise, nutrition, obesity, stress, and substance abuse.

EXERCISE Central to any physical fitness program is exercise. In elementary physical education, exercise can take many forms. Aerobic and anaerobic activities, calisthenics, sports activities, animal walks, dance, and other diverse forms of human movement can constitute exercise. *Exercise*, as defined in this book, is used to describe sustained large-muscle activity rather than highly specialized nonlocomotor movements. Exercise is a means to develop and maintain physical fitness. For children to attain optimal levels of fitness requires adherence to frequency, intensity, and time of activity (FIT). Chapters 2 and 5, respectively, provide a detailed explanation of the principles of exercise and exercise routines.

School programs that should emphasize exercise include: physical education, fitness testing, before- or afterschool sports, and scheduled physical activities for handicapped children. Youngsters can be motivated to participate in exercise through an appropriate award system, attractive bulletin boards, educational software, special programs emphasizing physical fitness, school demonstrations, periodic fitness assessment, and controlled competition.

Key Concepts

1. Fitness can be acquired only through muscular effort.
2. Fitness is a lifelong pursuit with habits formed during the elementary school years.
3. Development and maintenance of fitness requires a regular program that adheres to the principles of FIT.
4. Increasing the workload is the only way to improve fitness.
5. Cardiorespiratory fitness is improved through exercise of long duration.
6. To be effective, exercises must be done properly.
7. Static (slow) stretching, rather than ballistic (fast) stretching, is the recommended exercise procedure to improve flexibility.
8. Exercise is specific. To improve the fitness of a particular muscle (or group of muscles) requires exercising that muscle.
9. Especially during the elementary years, muscular strength is directly related to good posture.

Learning Experiences for Kindergarten Through Third Grade

1. Have children list different types of exercise. Put a blue dot next to activities that improve cardiovascular fitness and reduce body fat, a green dot next to activities that improve flexibility, and a yellow dot next to activities that improve muscular strength and endurance. Determine which exercises improve all components of health-related physical fitness.
2. Ask that students work with a partner and exercise before or after school. Discuss the value of exercising with a friend.
3. Introduce the skeletal and muscular systems of the body. Obtain bones, charts, x-rays, and other audiovisual resources to show the various bones and muscles of the body. Discuss how exercise affects the growth and development of the body.
4. Use word jumbles, dot-to-dots, word searches, crossword puzzles, and other instructional gimmicks to teach vocabulary associated with exercise.
5. Take the children on a field trip to a local health and fitness club. Arrange for a fitness instructor to lead the children through a typical workout. Introduce them to exercise bicycles, treadmills, and other equipment usually available in fitness facilities.

Learning Experiences for Fourth through Sixth Grade

1. Ask students to list activities they enjoy. Identify the components of fitness that are developed through participation in these favorite activities. Determine which activities enhance health-related fitness and which improve components of skill-related fitness.
2. Teach children how to calculate their target heart rate (Table 4–1). Identify exercises that allow them to attain the desired heart rate.
3. Have youngsters plan a personal exercise program. Ask them to keep a diary of their exercise routines. After several weeks, let them share their experiences with classmates.
4. Use various educational software to teach the principles and concepts of exercise. For additional information about available software contact: CompTech

Table 4-1 Formula and an Example for Calculating Target Heart Rates. (Example is for a 10-year-old child with a resting heart rate of 75 BPM.)

Step 1:	Formula for Calculating Maximal Heart Rate 220 – Age (in years) = Maximal Heart Rate	Example: 220 – 10 210 BPM
Step 2:	Formula for Calculating Working Heart Rate Maximal Heart Rate – Resting Heart Rate = Working Heart Rate	Example: 210 – 75 135
Step 3:	Formula for Calculating Threshold of Training Heart Rate Working Heart Rate * .60	Example: 135 * 60
		= 81
	+ Resting Heart Rate	+ 75
	= Threshold of Training Heart Rate	= 156
Step 4:	Formula for Calculating the Upper Limit of the Target Heart Rate Zone Working Heart Rate * .90	Example: 135 *.90
		= 121
	+ Resting Heart Rate	+ 75
	= Upper Limit for Target Heart Rate Zone	= 196

The target zone for this 10 year old child is 156-196.

Systems Design, P.O. Box 516, Hastings MN 55033; Edu-Tron, 3112 Waits Avenue, Fort Worth TX 76109.

5. Differentiate between aerobic and anaerobic exercise. Plan activities that help children feel the difference between the two types of exercise.

NUTRITION   Children's nutritional needs are much the same as those of adults. Youngsters require a high proportion of foods containing proper nourishment and energy for growth, maintenance, and repair of tissues, and for physical activity. Different amounts of these nutrients are essential to life. Proper nutrition is necessary if one is to obtain an optimum level of physical performance from one's body.

The elements in foods that are required for maintenance and growth of the body are called *nutrients*. Essential nutrients that provide energy (as measured in calories) are carbohydrates, proteins, and fats. Also essential, but needed in smaller amounts, are vitamins and minerals. These fundamental nutrients are found in the four basic food groups: (1) fruits and vegetables, (2) milk and milk products, (3) meat, fish, poultry with nuts and legumes as supplements, and (4) breads and cereals.

Children should learn about the elements of a balanced diet. While it is important to eat foods from the various food groups, moderation in the consumption of cholesterol and fats is advised. Excessive body fat makes the heart work much harder than normal and increases the chances of having high blood pressure. The ingestion of too much fat has been found to increase cholesterol and triglyceride levels in the blood. Results of recent scientific investigations have demonstrated a direct relationship between high cholesterol and triglyceride levels and the presence of coronary heart disease. Dietary sources high in cholesterol include cheese, eggs, butter, shrimp, sponge cake, pies, chocolate candy, ice cream, most beef and pork, and milk.

Since most childhood obesity is linked to overeating and inactivity, it is important to teach children about the caloric content of food (in addition to the nutritional values). To offset excessive caloric consumption, youngsters need to learn to monitor the amount of calories ingested and the amount of calories burned by different types of physical activity.

Key Concepts

1. The American public is food conscious, but not very nutrition conscious.

2. Excessive body fat, due in part to poor dietary habits, has become increasingly prevalent in children.

3. There are numerous myths and misinformation about what foods do.

4. To ensure that the body is receiving essential nutrients, the diet should be balanced and contain foods from each of the four food groups.

5. Fad diets are a poor means of weight control and may contribute to health problems.

6. Necessary caloric consumption depends on age, sex, size, muscle mass, glandular function, emotional state, climate, and amount of physical activity (Table 4-2).

7. Physically active children do not need more protein than sedentary children.

8. Weight maintenance is best achieved through a combination of caloric reduction and energy expenditure.

9. Junk foods are usually high in calories and low in nutritional value.

10. Excessive consumption of fat increases the chance of heart disease.

11. Physical activities vary in energy expenditure. Individual needs must be considered in the selection of exercise activities.

Learning Experiences for Kindergarten Through Third Grade

1. Have children measure their height and weight. Continue this on a monthly basis for the entire school year.

2. Cut out pictures of food from magazines. Select pictures that show one kind of food. See if the children can sort the pictures into the four basic food groups. Then make a poster of the pictures.

3. Ask children to plan three meals for their families. Be sure they include essential foods from each of the four groups. Do not forget to include drinks.

4. Introduce children to cookbooks. Let them become familiar with the terms calorie, carbohydrates, minerals, protein, and other nutritional terms.

5. Make a breakfast suggestion box. Ask children to bring breakfast recipes from home. Use this to develop a breakfast menu.

Learning Experiences for Fourth Through Sixth Grade

1. Familiarize students with microcomputer software that is designed to teach the concepts and principles of proper nutrition. For additional information

Table 4-2 Recommended Daily Dietary Allowances for Children Ages 6-12

Age	Calories	Protein (gm)	Calcium (gm)	Iron (mg)	Vitamin A (I.U.)	Thiamin (mg)	Riboflavin (mg)	Niacin (mg)	Vitamin C (mg)
6-8	2000	35	0.9	10	3500	1.0	1.1	13	40
8-10	2100	40	1.0	10	3500	1.1	1.2	15	40
10-12 (boys)	2500	45	1.2	10	4500	1.3	1.3	17	40
10-12 (girls)	2250	50	1.2	18	4500	1.1	1.3	15	40

Source: U.S. Department of Agriculture, "Nutritive Value of Foods." *Home and Garden*, Bulletin 72, 1976, p. 40.

Table 4-3 Foods Recommended for Daily Diets of Children Ages 6-12

Food Group	Food Source	Quantity
Meats	Meat, poultry, fish	2-4 oz.
	Second protein dish: small serving meat, legumes, or nuts	4-6 tbsp.
	Eggs	1 whole egg
Vegetables and fruits	Potatoes (or equivalent amount of rice, macaroni, spaghetti)	1 medium to large, or 4-5 tbsp.
	Other cooked vegetables (green leafy or deep yellow) frequently	4-5 tbsp at one or more meals
	Raw vegetables (carrots, lettuce, celery, etc.)	1/4 to 1/3 cup
	Vitamin C food (citrus fruits, tomatoes, etc.)	1 medium orange or equivalent
	Other fruits	1/2 c. or more at one or more meals
Bread and cereal	Cereal (whole-grain, restored, or enriched)	3/4 c. or more
Milk	Milk (or equivalent)	1 1/2 pt. (2-3 c.)
Miscellaneous	Butter or fortified margarine	1 tbsp. or more
	Sweets	1/2 c. simple dessert at 1 or 2 meals

Source: From Jean L. Bogert, George M. Briggs, and Doris H. Calloway, *Nutrition and Physical Fitness* (9th Ed.). Philadelphia: W.B. Saunders.

about available software contact: CompTech Systems Design, P.O. Box 516, Hastings MN 55033; Edu-Tron, 3112 Waits Avenue, Fort Worth TX 76109.

2. Have children plan and prepare meals. Be sure that all food groups are represented in the meals (Table 4-3). Encourage children to ask their parents for an opportunity to cook at home.

3. Talk with adults about the ways foods and access to foods has changed since they were growing up. Discuss the differences between fast foods and traditional meals.

4. Conduct simulated grocery shopping experiences. Give children play money to buy groceries for one week. Analyze the purchases in terms of nutritional requirements, food group representation, and cost effectiveness.

OBESITY Physical attractiveness is one of the primary reasons individuals are concerned about weight control. Desirable weight is usually derived from charts that base estimations on height, age, and sex. While weight charts are good guidelines, it is becoming more apparent that height-weight tables are not as accurate an indication of health as body composition.

While tables that convert millimeters of skinfold thickness to percentage body fat have been readily available for adults, only recently has it been possible to accurately translate sum of skinfold to percentage of body fat in children. The ability to accurately predict children's body composition makes more meaningful the skinfold test and represents a milestone in fitness evaluation. Figures 2–8 and 2–9 offer acceptable levels for skinfold measurements that are related to good health.

Key Concepts

1. Overfat is different from overweight and is more important in determining health.

2. Obesity is a national health concern affecting all segments of our society.

3. Obesity increases the risk of heart disease and related health problems.

4. Weight is not necessarily an accurate measure of obesity. Skinfold calipers that measure thickness of body fat should be used to determine percentage of body fat.

5. Responding to overfatness by excessive dieting can be dangerous and lead to serious health problems.

6. Obese children often experience physical activities in ways different from children of normal weight.

7. Obesity impedes skill acquisition.

8. Exercise and vigorous physical activity are effective means of controlling body fat.

9. Sustained exercise for long periods of time is perhaps the best way to reduce body fat.

10. Fat children usually become fat adults.

Learning Experiences for Kindergarten Through Third Grade

1. Show the children a jar of chicken fat. Inform them that this is how fat looks in their bodies.

2. Create bulletin boards that show pictures of obese adults. Discuss the importance of developing a lean physique early in life.

3. Have children learn to use low-cost skinfold calipers. Teach them how to measure each other's skinfold thickness.

4. Many educational materials teach concepts of obesity, including workbooks, coloring books, and other media. The Fitness Finders Feelin' Good Program (133 Teft Road, P.O. Box 507, Spring Arbor MI 49283) is a popular clearinghouse for fitness materials.

5. Use the microcomputer to develop word searches, crossword puzzles, dot-to-dots, and assorted other games with obesity as the theme.

Learning Experiences for Fourth Through Sixth Grade

1. Explain the difference between body weight and percentage of body fat. Emphasize the importance of using percentage of body fat as an indicator of health.

2. From the sum of skinfolds (triceps and subscapular) determine percentage of body fat. Have children convert percentage of fat into pounds of fat (actually, body weight × percentage of fat). To show how this unnecessary fat burdens the body and inhibits movement, have youngsters carry a book bag or back pack of equal weight for an entire school day.

3. Introduce children to caloric expenditure tables. Ask them to see how many calories can be burned by participating in their favorite physical activity (Table 4–4).

4. Analyze the activity levels of other students in and out of class. Estimate the caloric expenditure of those observed.

5. Ask children to keep a record of their physical activity and caloric consumption for a week. At the end of the week, have them determine the difference between energy expended and calories consumed.

6. Discuss the ways society rewards physically fit individuals, and contrast this with the ways in which obese children are sometimes treated by teachers and classmates.

STRESS

The term *stress* is used frequently to describe a person's reaction to the demands of modern society. Stress can be a pleasant or unpleasant motivating force that creates feelings of tension that can cause physiological or psychological changes in the human body. Physical responses to stress are increased heart rate, increased blood pressure, increased respiration rate, increased muscle tension, and decreased digestive functions. In children, minor ailments such as headaches, stomach aches, back aches, loss of appetite, and irritability may also appear.

Psychologically, stress can take the form of excitement, fear, or anger. The inability to relieve stress through productive means during childhood may lead to substance abuse in adulthood. Sources of stress for children include unrealistically high expectations imposed by parents, the educational environment, frustration due to the thwarting of desires, perceived personal inadequacies,

Table 4-4 Minutes of Activity Needed to Burn Up Food Calories

Calories	Food	Sedentary	Light	Moderate	Vigorous	Strenuous
630	Burger King Whopper	543	252	126	84	63
541	McDonald's Big Mac	466	216	108	72	54
258	Burger Chef Hamburger	222	103	52	34	26
440	Arthur Treacher's Fish Sandwich	379	176	88	59	44
402	McDonald's Filet-O-Fish	347	161	80	54	40
409	Long John Silver's Fish (2 pcs.)	353	164	82	55	41
830	Kentucky Fried Original Recipe Three Piece Dinner	716	332	166	111	83
950	Kentucky Fried Extra-Crispy Three Piece Dinner	819	380	190	127	95
340	Pizza Hut Thin 'n Crispy Cheese Pizza (half 13″ pie)	293	136	68	45	34
450	Pizza Hut Thick 'n Chewy Pepperoni Pizza (half 10″ pie)	388	180	90	60	45
352	McDonald's Egg McMuffin	303	141	70	47	35
186	Taco Bell Taco	160	74	37	25	19
270	Dairy Queen Brazier Hot Dog	233	108	54	36	27
210	Burger King French Fries	181	84	42	28	21
300	Dairy Queen Onion Rings	259	120	60	40	30
340	Burger King Vanilla Shake	293	136	68	45	34
364	McDonald's Chocolate Shake	314	146	72	49	36
300	McDonald's Apple Pie	259	120	60	40	30
15	2—8-inch Celery Stalks	13	6	3	2	1
55	2 Medium Graham Crackers	47	22	11	7	6
105	2 teaspoons Peanuts	91	42	21	14	11
145	1 cup Plain Low Fat Yogurt	125	58	29	19	15
225	1 cup Fruit Flavored Yogurt	194	90	45	30	23
430	12 ounce Chocolate Milkshake	371	172	86	57	43

Source: From C. T. Kuntzleman, *The Beat Goes On.* Arbor, Michigan: Arbor Press, 1980.

self-imposed pressures to succeed, or conflict arising from having to choose between alternatives. Realistic, challenging, and attainable goals tend to eliminate many frustrating, potentially stressful situations.

Children need to understand that stress-induced changes in bodily function can either inhibit or enhance physical performance. Teaching children how to recognize stressful symptoms and manage stress are essential elements to achieving a productive and healthy outlook on life. Developing effective methods of coping with stress can be considered preventive medicine.

Individuals who most effectively deal with stress seem to go through a certain process. This four-phase approach to handling stress is as follows:

1. *Evaluating the situation.* An accurate appraisal of the situation is conducted. Relying on past experiences and current perceptions assists in formulating a true picture. Distorting the facts may decrease a person's chances of coping with the stressful situation.

2. *Determining alternatives.* Rational decisions grow out of constructive thought. Therefore, alternative actions must be formulated from a logical, conscious process. The ultimate course of action depends on the probabilities of success, the degree of satisfaction one will accept, and the price one is willing to pay.

3. *Making an action response.* Acting on a decision requires complete commitment on the part of the child. The timing of making an action-related decision and the context in which the decision is made are also important considerations associated with stress reduction. Youngsters should only act when confidence is high and all available alternatives have been evaluated. Delaying action may be just as stress producing as acting too soon.

4. *Utilizing feedback.* If an action receives positive feedback, the outcome is reinforced and stress is reduced. If the action yields negative feedback, it is likely to increase stress and should be questioned. In either case, using feedback to assess decisions is helpful in preparing for future action decisions.

Key Concepts

1. Stress is an unavoidable product of our fast-paced society and can be either productive or detrimental.

2. A certain amount of stress is necessary to stimulate performance.

3. Stress affects all people, regardless of age.

4. Many times, substance abuse or other unhealthy behaviors are the result of unsuccessful attempts to deal with stress.

5. Stress can cause alterations to bodily functions that may increase susceptibility to diseases.

6. Improper perceptions of our responsibilities may induce stress.

7. Stress interferes with our responses to normal everyday occurrences.

8. Changing goals, diversifying activities, and equating work and play can contribute to stress reduction.

9. Individuals react differently to stressful situations.

10. Vigorous physical activity is an excellent way to reduce stress and tension.

11. It is important to learn to live with personal expectations, not the expectations of others.

Learning Experiences for Kindergarten Through Third Grade

1. Ask students to identify stressors. Discuss those they have experienced.

2. Select a locomotor movement. Ask children to identify the muscles necessary to complete the movement and those that can be relaxed.

3. Discuss how different emotions (i.e., anger, happiness, sadness, etc.) affect the body.

4. Introduce relaxation techniques that may temporarily alleviate stress.

5. Ask children to perform a simple motor task. Then ask them to perform a skill they are unable to perform. What feelings were experienced during the performance of each?

Learning Experiences for Fourth Through Sixth Grade

1. Identify situations in physical education that provoke stress. Include events such as unfair play, unsafe movement, and discourteous behavior, as well as competitive situations.

2. Ask an athlete to speak to the class about controlling stress in highly competitive sporting contests.

3. Discuss alternatives to stress reduction. Include the use of drugs and other unhealthy practices in the conversation.

4. Try to determine the relationship between physical activity and stress reduction.

5. Discuss the importance of realistic goal setting in managing stress. Ask students to determine a practice sequence that will conclude with the performance of a previously unlearned complex skill. Have students identify the various types of stressors encountered during the learning of the task.

SUBSTANCE ABUSE

Drug abuse occurs when a substance deliberately is not taken for its intended purpose. Continued abuse usually results in some long-term physical, psychological, or social problem. By no means an accepted pattern of behavior among the majority of the American public, the abuse of tobacco, alcohol, and other recreational drugs is quite common among elementary school youngsters.

Facts about substance abuse should be presented to children without moralizing or preaching. Children need to know the impact of substance abuse on the healthy body. Wise and sensible decisions regarding the use of drugs usually result from understanding the facts about the short- and long-term effects of substance abuse. Substance abuse is so contrary to the concept of wellness that elementary physical educators must accept the challenge to increase awareness of the problem.

Key Concepts

1. Drugs are medical tools that have many benefits when properly used.
2. There is a wide variety of drugs and other substances which, if misused, may be harmful.
3. Behavior patterns are established during the formative years and usually influence a person's life style.
4. There are laws that control the production, distribution, and use of drugs.
5. American society is responsible for the control of drug abuse.
6. The earlier one begins to abuse drugs, the greater the risk to functional health.
7. Individuals choose to abuse drugs for reasons of curiosity, status, and peer pressure.
8. Practicing a healthful life style different from peers requires courage. Feeling good about oneself is more important than being accepted by peers.
9. Exercise and a physically active life style are more productive ways to cope with problems than drugs.
10. Smoking constricts the blood vessels and causes the pulse rate to increase by 10 to 20 beats per minute.

Learning Experiences for Kindergarten Through Third Grade

1. Invite a school nurse to talk about the hazards of drugs.
2. Discuss the type of information a doctor needs to prescribe drugs.
3. Ask the students to draw pictures of proper places to store medication.
4. Talk about the effects of smoking and alcohol consumption on a healthy body.
5. Identify the many forms of physical and psychological harm that result from drug abuse.
6. Discuss some of the social problems created by alcohol abuse.
7. Develop visuals (bulletin boards, mobiles, puzzles, etc.) that depict healthy and unhealthy life styles.

Learning Experiences for Fourth Through Sixth Grade

1. Invite a former smoker or alcoholic to speak to the class about his or her personal experiences with drugs.
2. Discuss the importance of being your own person and making wise and meaningful decisions.
3. Use role playing to place the children in decision-making situations.
4. Children are influenced by television ads depicting professional athletes using alcohol. Discuss the reasons why these elite athletes are able to perform at high levels of physical performance while using alcohol.
5. As a homework assignment, ask the students to write a report on the various diseases linked to abuse of tobacco and/or alcohol.
6. Conduct value-clarification sessions to discuss how individuals should learn to make decisions about themselves without being influenced by peers.

7. Invite a doctor to speak about the physiological effects of substance abuse on performance.

8. Make some of the many media packages and visual aids depicting the results of substance abuse available to students.

9. Discuss the value of a physically active life style in reducing tension.

10. Discuss the economic impact drug use has on American society. Look at work days lost, legal costs, property losses, accidents, rehabilitation expenses, and other cost factors.

References

AAHPERD. (1976). *AAHPERD Youth Fitness Test Manual.* Reston VA: Author.

AAHPERD. (1988). *AAHPERD Physical Best Test Manual.* Reston VA: Author.

Cumming, C. B. (1975). The child in sport and physical activity: Medical comment. In J. G. Albinson & G. M. Andrews (Eds.), *Child in Sport and Physical Activity.* Baltimore MD: University Park Press.

Gilliam, T. B., Freedson, P. S., Geenen, D. L., & Shahraray, B. (1981). Physical activity patterns determined by heart rate monitoring in 6–7 year-old children. *Medicine and Science in Sports and Exercise, 9,* 21–25.

Hastad, D. N., & Pangrazi, R. P. (1983). Summer alterations in youth fitness. *The Physical Educator, 40,* 81–87.

Hovell, M., Bursick, J., Sharkey, R., & McClure, J. (1978). An evaluation of elementary students' voluntary physical activity during recess. *Research Quarterly, 49,* 460–474.

Macek, M., & Vavra, J. (1974). Prolonged exercise in children. *Acta Paediatrica Belgica, 28,* 13–18.

Suggested Supplementary References

Arizona Department of Education. (1982). *Sports Nutrition.* [(20 U.S.C. 122le-3(a)(1)]. Phoenix AZ: Department of Education.

AAHPERD. (1984). *Technical Manual: Health Related Physical Fitness.* Reston VA.: Author.

Corbin, C. B., & Lindsey, R. (1983). *Fitness for Life.* Glenview IL: Scott, Foresman and Company.

Corbin, C. B., & Lindsey, R. (1988). *Concepts of Physical Fitness with Laboratories.* Dubuque IA: Wm. C. Brown.

Dauer, V. P., & Pangrazi, R. P. (1989). *Dynamic Physical Education for Elementary School Children.* (9th ed.). New York: Macmillan.

Engs, R., & Wantz, M. (1978). *Teaching Health Education in the Elementary School.* Boston: Houghton Mifflin.

Ensor, P. G., Means, R. K., & Henkel, B. M. (1985). *Personal Health: Appraising Behavior.* New York: John Wiley & Sons.

Harcourt Brace Jovanovich, Publishers. (1983). *HBJ Health* (Vols. Orange, Purple, & Brown). New York: Author.

Kuntzleman, C. T. (1977). *Heartbeat.* Spring Arbor MI: Arbor Press.

Kuntzleman, C. T. (1978). *Fitness Discovery Activities.* Spring Arbor MI: Arbor Press.

CHAPTER FIVE

Fitness Activities and Routines

"**W**hen all is said and done, usually more is said than done." Hopefully, this is not the motto describing the implementation of fitness activities for children. This chapter was written to provide practitioners with information, activities, and tips necessary to begin incorporating a balanced approach to physical fitness into the daily lesson. The following sections discuss strategies for implementing a year-long fitness program, exercises for total body development, exercise precautions, suggested fitness routines, and fitness adaptations for sports skills and games.

Implementing Physical Fitness Activities

The following points are described with brevity since they have been covered in greater detail in previous chapters. When developing fitness workouts for youngsters, remember that **FIT** is a useful acronym for remembering the rules for fitness prescription. *F*requency is the number of times per week fitness activities should be performed. Three times per week is the recommended minimum. *I*ntensity of cardiovascular exercise can be monitored by teaching children to check their heart rates. The training rate is reached when the heart rate is elevated into the training zone and maintained for a minimum of 10 minutes. *T*ime is the length of each exercise bout. A typical physical education period is 30 minutes in length. At least 10 minutes of the period should be devoted to activity that elevates the heart rate into the training zone as described above.

Progression must be followed when teaching fitness activities to children. The typical stereotype for physical fitness instruction has been the "daily dozen and run-a-mile" approach. This defeats everything known about individualized instruction. There is tremendous variation among children in terms of physical capacity (see Chapter 1) which necessitates teaching to these differences. One of the most effective ways of turning children off to exercise for a lifetime is to ask them to do more than they are capable of performing. Keep initial demands low and gradually increase the workload. In order to allow for differing capacities, organize activities so children do not have to start and finish at the same time. Begin the year with demands that are low enough to assure all children experience success. The "battle may be won but the war is lost" if children cultivate a negative attitude toward activity due to excessive workloads placed on them by an overenthusiastic instructor.

Assure that a wide variety of fitness activities are offered children. Youngsters often tire of the same activities and it is well established that motivation to exercise is decreased when children perceive the activities to be boring. Second, most adults who exercise have a favorite type of exercise. It is reasonable to think that children should be taught that there are many "roads to fitness" and that no single type of exercise is best for all people. Teach children a number of ways of exercising for fitness and how to modify each way to assure that fitness benefits will accrue.

Fitness and Class Management

The amount of time available for physical fitness instruction is usually limited so teachers must effectively utilize time within the physical fitness section of the lesson. It is possible to manage a class efficiently using movement activities that simultaneously enhance the youngsters' fitness levels. This approach emphasizes quick and efficient methods for moving, grouping, and pairing children for fitness activity.

FINDING A PARTNER
A simple game of Back to Back (Dauer & Pangrazi, 1989) can be used for pairing youngsters. An added advantage of the activity is that it can be used to practice management skills as well as develop cardiovascular fitness. Children are instructed to move throughout the area and get back to back with a partner as quickly as possible. Students who don't find a partner in the vicinity run to the center of the area and raise their hands. Other children will be available as partners. If there is an extra child, the teacher can assign him or her to another pair or serve as the child's partner. This activity can be varied by changing the locomotor movement (skip, hop, gallop, etc.) as well as the position (toe to toe, elbow to elbow, etc.). The focus of the activity is learning to make the nearest person a partner as quickly as possible. This avoids the practice of looking for a friend or telling someone they are not wanted as a partner. It also minimizes the amount of time needed for choosing a partner. As an additional stipulation, ask students to choose someone who is their own height, weight, strength, etc. This is especially useful when exercises demand a partner of equal size and weight.

Many different challenges can be added, such as find a friend (1) who is wearing the same color as you, (2) who has a birthday in the same month as you, (3) who has the same color eyes, and so on.

BREAKING INTO SMALL GROUPS
Small groups are used for many of the suggested fitness routines. An enjoyable management and fitness game used to form small groups is Whistle Mixer (Dauer & Pangrazi, 1989). Youngsters move (any specified locomotor movement) around the area. The instructor blows a whistle a certain number of times to specify the group size. Students quickly form groups based on the number of whistle blasts (four blasts means groups of four). When the specified number of students is in the group, they are required to sit down. For added excitement, it can be specified that the first group with the correct number and sitting down is the winner.

An advantage of using this activity is that it gives the teacher a rapid, easy way to organize children into groups of different sizes. Teachers and students should realize that management skills demand practice similar to all other skills.

DIVIDING THE CLASS IN HALF
It is common to divide a class in half to play many of the fitness games and sport drills. An easy way to do so is to signal the class to get back to back. Ask one partner to sit down while the other remains standing. Move the standing players

first to one side of the area. Then ask the sitting players to move to the opposite side.

MOVING INTO FORMATIONS   Students often enjoy performing activities in various formations. Many instructors like to place their class into a circle for various fitness routines. As is the case in all practice of management skills, ask the class to move throughout the area. On the command "rectangle," the class silently moves into a rectangular formation. The instructor can ask the shape to be made a specified number of steps larger or smaller. An element of excitement can be added by dividing the class in half and seeing who can make the formation first and with the highest quality (straight lines, full circle, etc.).

Teachers often ask students to make a circle—the hardest of all formations to construct. Placing four cones in a square or rectangular shape will serve as the corners and make it much easier in the learning stages of this approach. Remember that all circle activities can be done just as easily in square or rectangular formation.

CIRCLE FORMATION   Since many activities are done in circle formation, an easy and active method for forming such a shape should be taught. An easy way is to ask students to "fall in" behind another person while moving throughout the area. As all students move into place behind one another, a large circle will result. The teacher can then move into the circle and enlarge or reduce the size of the circle as desired. If multiple circles occur, remind the class that one large circle is the desired result. When a circle is needed, it becomes very easy to tell the students to move, fall in, and freeze when the circle is complete.

All the methods above use the basic locomotor movements to initiate action. Most warm-up activities can be done by moving throughout the area into the desired formation. This allows the teacher to make a smooth transition from warm-up into the desired formation, with students ready for fitness activity. A side benefit is that there is much less off-task behavior when students are moving in contrast to standing around, talking, counting off, and moving into position.

Fitness and the Physical Education Lesson

Physical fitness activities are one part of a total physical education lesson. Physical education should encompass fitness *and* skill development. Ignoring skill instruction in order to offer an extended period of fitness development is strongly discouraged. Physical skills are often the tools that adults use to maintain physical fitness. It is important to include fitness instruction in every lesson. Too often, teachers eliminate fitness from the day's activities due to a lack of time. This implies that the teacher (and school) do not value physical fitness. Even when physical education is offered only one day per week, fitness should be included so youngsters understand that fitness is an important component of physical participation.

Fitness instruction should be preceded by a 2- to 3-minute warm-up period. There are many methods of warming up, such as stretching, walking and slow jogging, and performing various exercises at a slower than usual pace. It is important that youngsters be offered the opportunity to "loosen up" and prepare their bodies for more strenuous activity to assure that they develop proper exercise habits.

The fitness portion of the daily lesson, including warm-up, should not extend much beyond 10 to 12 minutes. Some might argue that more time is needed to develop adequate fitness. Undoubtedly, a higher level of fitness could be developed if more time were devoted to the area. However, the reality of the situation is that most teachers are offered 20- to 30-minute periods of instruction. Since skill instruction is part of a balanced physical education program, it is necessary to make some compromises to assure that all phases of the program are covered.

If one accepts that approximately 2 to 3 minutes are allowed for warm-up activity and 10 minutes for fitness, the importance of effectively and efficiently using the time becomes obvious. After an initial period of instruction, fitness activity should be continuous and demanding. Heart rates should be elevated into the target heart rate zone. Class management skills should be effectively used to assure that students are on task. In the upper grades, students can lead the activity while the teacher moves throughout the area and offers individualized instruction. Participation and instruction should be enthusiastic and focus on positive outcomes. If the instructor does not enjoy physical fitness participation, such an attitude will be apparent to students. Above all, fitness activities should *never* be assigned as punishment. This teaches students that "push-ups, running, and so forth" are things you do when you misbehave. The opportunity to exercise should be a privilege and an enjoyable experience. Think of the money adults spend in order to exercise. Take a positive approach and offer students the chance to walk or jog with a friend when they do something well. This not only allows them the opportunity to visit with a friend, but to exercise on a positive note. Be an effective salesperson; sell the joy of activity and benefits of physical fitness to youngsters.

The Fitness Module

The fitness module is that portion of the daily lesson dedicated exclusively to the presentation of a wide variety of fitness activities. The following are suggestions to aid in the successful implementation of the fitness module:

1. Activities should be vigorous in nature, exercise all body parts, and cover the major components of fitness. All children are capable of strenuous workloads geared to their age, fitness level, and abilities. To be successful, exercises must adhere to **FIT** and other principles of exercise and be within the capabilities of students.

2. Novel fitness routines comprised of sequential exercises for total body development are recommended alternatives to a year-long program of regimented calisthenics. A diverse array of routines that appeal to the interest and fitness level of the children should replace the somewhat traditional approach of doing the same routine day in and day out. The following sections of this chapter describe various fitness activities that can be used for children in the primary and intermediate grades.

3. The fitness routine should be conducted during the first part of the lesson. Relegating fitness to the end of the lesson does little to enhance the image of exercise. Further, by having the exercise phase of the lesson precede skill instruction, the concept, "You get fit to play sport, you don't play sport to get fit" is reinforced.

4. The teacher should assume an active role. Children respond positively to role modeling. A teacher who actively exercises with children, hustles to assist those youngsters having difficulty performing selected exercises, and is able to make exercise fun begins to instill in children the value of an active life style.

5. Various forms of audio or visual assistance should be used to increase children's level of motivation. Background music, colorful posters depicting exercises, tambourine or drum assistance to provide rhythmical accompaniment for activity, and other instructional media aids can assist in making vigorous activity more enjoyable.

6. The variety of fitness activities used in the module should be changed on a regular basis. To maintain the students' interest and further increase their knowledge about exercise, activities, and routines that encourage total fitness development should be varied at regular intervals. Given the many exercises and activities available to develop fitness, this is not difficult.

7. When introducing a new activity, show children how it is to be done and identify it with a specific name. State the purpose of the exercise and its value. Help children through the exercise in parts until the sequence of movement is mastered.

8. When developing workloads for children, the two available alternatives are time and repetitions. It may be more effective to base the number of exercise repetitions on time, rather than a specified amount since this will allow the children to set personal limits within the time frame. Limits based on the capacity of each individual are most effective, but more difficult to administer. Having the class perform as many sit-ups as possible in the time given will result in more children working at or near their potential than asking the entire class to complete 15 sit-ups. Note that both time and repetitions are listed with each of the sample fitness routines in this chapter. This allows the teacher to make a decision as to the most effective approach for the particular setting.

THE YEARLY PLAN   Following is a suggested yearly plan of fitness instruction. It is offered as an example for planning the year's activities. Developing a yearly plan is important to assure that a wide variety of experiences are offered to learners. It also allows progression to be planned for and assures that youngsters will receive a well-rounded program of instruction. An important point to remember is that physical fitness instruction must be planned in a manner similar to the skill development component of the lesson. For too long, little thought and concern has been given to fitness. Small wonder that youngsters grow up thinking that physical fitness can be achieved *only* through running laps and doing calisthenics.

When organizing a yearly plan for fitness instruction (Table 5–1), consider some of the following points: Units of fitness instruction should vary in length depending on the age of the youngsters. Primary-grade children need to experience a wide variety of routines in order to maintain a high level of motivation. During these years, exposure to many different types of activities is more important than a progressive, demanding fitness routine. The first experiences of fitness instruction must be positive and enjoyable. As children mature, units can be extended to 2 weeks. In the fifth and sixth grades, units of 3 weeks allow for progression and overload to occur within units. In spite of the varying length of units, one principle must be followed: *There are many methods for developing fitness, none of which is best for ALL children.* Offer a wide variety of routines and activities so youngsters learn that fitness is not lockstep and unbending. The yearly plan should offer activities that allow all types of youngsters to find success at one time or another during the school year.

The yearly plan reveals another important criteria to consider when developing a fitness program. The routines become much more structured as youngsters grow older. Most of the activities listed for kindergarten through second grade are unstructured and allow for a wide variation of performance. For older children, emphasis on proper technique and performance increases. However, this is not to imply that every student must do every activity exactly the same. It is unrealistic to think that an obese youngster will be able to perform at a level similar to a lean child. Allow for variation of performance while emphasizing the importance of "doing your best."

Physical Fitness Activities

The following physical fitness activities are ordered from unstructured to structured and designed to be placed into the fitness module of the lesson. Refer

Table 5-1 Sample Yearly Fitness Plan

Grades K-2	Grades 3-4	Grades 5-6
1. Slow, Medium Fast	Slow, Medium, Fast	Student Leader Exercises
2. Challenge Activities	Fitness Games	Student Leader Exercises
3. Challenge Activities	Fitness Games	Student Leader Exercises
4. Jogging	Jogging	Continuous Movement Drills
5. Combination Movements	Continuous Movement Drills	Continuous Movement Drills
6. Fitness Games	Continuous Movement Drills	Continuous Movement Drills
7. Fitness Testing	Fitness Testing	Fitness Testing
8. Animal Movements	Sport Related Fitness Activity	Fitness Games
9. Hexagon Hustle	Parachute Activities	Parachute Activities
10. Parachute Activities	Parachute Activities	Parachute Activities
11. Challenge Activities	Interval Training	Sport Related Fitness Activity
12. Teacher Leader Exercises	Exercises to Music	Sport Related Fitness Activity
13. Exercises to Music	Exercises to Music	Jogging
14. Obstacle Course	Rope Jumping	Circuit Training
15. Combination Movements	Circuit Training	Circuit Training
16. Circuit Training	Circuit Training	Circuit Training
17. Continuous Movement Drills	Obstacle Course	Aerobic Dance
18. Animal Movements	Rope Jumping and Exercise	Aerobic Dance
19. Rope Jumping and Exercise	Rope Jumping and Exercise	Aerobic Dance
20. Circuit Training	Fitness Games	Interval Training
21. Challenge Activities	Aerobic Dance	Jogging
22. Fitness Games	Aerobic Dance	Jogging
23. Exercises to Music	Jogging	Student Leader Exercises
24. Combination Movements	Student Leader Exercises	Student Leader Exercises
25. Hexagon Hustle	Student Leader Exercises	Student Leader Exercises
26. Parachute Activities	Parachute Activities	Hexagon Hustle
27. Rope Jumping	Hexagon Hustle	Hexagon Hustle
28. Aerobic Dance	Hexagon Hustle	Hexagon Hustle
29. Fitness Testing	Fitness Testing	Fitness Testing
30. Rope Jumping and Exercise	Interval Training	Interval Training
31. Animal Movements	Exercises to Music	Obstacle Course
32. Exercises to Music	Exercises to Music	Obstacle Course
33. Aerobic Dance	Sport Related Fitness Activities	Fitness Games
34. Hexagon Hustle	Grass Drills and Partner Resistance	Grass Drills and Partner Resistance
35. Grass Drills and Exercises	Grass Drills and Partner Resistance	Grass Drills and Partner Resistance

to Table 5-1 to determine the recommended number of weeks each activity or routine should be taught.

SLOW, MEDIUM, FAST MOVEMENTS

A whistle is used to signal students to change from one tempo of locomotor movement to another. For example, if students were assigned walking as the locomotor movement, one whistle would signal a slow walk, two whistles a medium walk, and three whistles a fast walk. Different locomotor movements such as running, skipping, galloping, and sliding can be used for variation.

At regular intervals, students can stop and perform various stretching activities and exercises. This will allow short rest periods between bouts of activity. Examples of activities might include a one-leg balance, push-ups, sit-ups, touching the toes, and any other challenges.

TEACHING HINT

Alternate nonlocomotor activities with locomotor activities. When youngsters are pushed too hard aerobically, they will express their fatigue in many different manners, i.e., complaining, quitting, misbehaving, and sitting out. Effective fitness instructors are keenly aware of how far to push and when to ease up. Instruction must be sensitive to the capacities of youngsters!

CHALLENGE ACTIVITIES

Children of all ages respond to challenges. Many different activities can be used to challenge youngsters to move toward various fitness goals. Much of the success of this approach centers on how the teacher presents various challenges. Youngsters must feel the enthusiasm of the teacher as he or she encourages them to perform and accomplish the task. The following are examples of movement challenges that can be used to exercise various parts of the body. Remember, these are just suggestions and many more can be developed by both students and teacher. A combination of movements from different areas should be put together so children exercise the major parts of the body, i.e., upper body, abdominal region, legs, and cardiovascular system.

Arm-Shoulder Girdle Development

- Can you walk on your hands and feet?
- Can you walk on two hands and one foot?
- Can you walk on one hand and one foot?
- Can you walk in the crab position (tummy toward the ceiling)?
- In crab position, can you wave an arm at a friend? Can you wave a foot at a friend?
- How long can you hold a bridge (i.e., push-up) position?
- Who can walk to this line in the push-up position?
- Who can scratch their back with the right hand while maintaining the push-up position?
- Can anyone clap their hands while holding the push-up position?
- Starting in the push-up position, walk the feet to the hands and back to the original position. Who can walk just one foot forward?
- From the push-up position, lower the body 1 inch at a time. How many of you can move 5 inches?
- From the push-up position, who can turn over and face the ceiling?

Abdominal Development

- In a sitting position, who can pick up one leg and shake it? Who can pick up both legs and shake them?
- In a sitting position, who can lean the upper body backward without falling? How long can you hold this position?
- From a sitting position, who can lower themselves slowly to the floor? Now, can you sit up?
- In a supine position, who can lift their head and look at their toes? Can you see your heels? Who can see the back of their knees?
- In a supine position, who can "wave" a leg at a friend? Use the other leg. Use both legs.
- From a supine position, who can sit up and touch their toes?
- From a supine position, who can hold their shoulders off the floor?
- From a sitting position, who can lift their legs off the floor and at the same time touch their toes with their fingers?
- From a supine position, who can sit up with hands placed on tummy? With hands folded across the chest? With hands placed on the top of the head?

Legs and Aerobic Activity

- Who can run in place? Who can do 50 running steps in place without stopping?
- Who can do 40 skips or gallops?

- Who can slide all the way around the gymnasium?
- Who can hop 30 times on the left foot?
- Who can jump in place 40 times?
- Who can jump in place while twisting the arms and upper body?
- Who can do 10 skips, 10 gallops, and finish with 30 running steps?
- Who can hold hands with a partner and do 100 jumps?
- Who can jump the rope 50 times?
- Who can hop back and forth over this line from one end of the gym to the other?
- Try to run as fast as you can. How long can you keep going?

COMBINATION MOVEMENTS

The focus should be on combining different types of locomotor movements with nonlocomotor movements. Locomotor movements include walking, running, skipping, galloping, hopping, jumping, leaping, and sliding. Nonlocomotor movements include twisting, turning, rolling, rocking, bending, swinging, stretching, pushing, and pulling. Overload and progression can be developed by increasing the amount of time devoted to the locomotor movements and reducing the amount of nonlocomotor movement. Movements can be stimulated by following the leader, announcing the sequence, or encouraging students to develop their own sequences. Following is an example of putting different combinations together in developing a fitness module for kindergarteners through second graders.

- Run, freeze, and stretch.
- Skip, jump in place, and twist in 4 different ways.
- Perform 30 slide steps, change direction every 5 slides.
- Gallop, find a partner, and pull–stretch with a partner.
- Try to do 35 skips, 20 hops, stop, and do 3 different types of rocking movements.
- Balance on one body part, swing with a partner, and run sideways throughout the area.
- Run, leap, roll, and rock. Repeat the sequence 5 times.
- Develop a sequence that includes walking, moving backwards, changing directions, stretching, and twisting. How many different sequences can you think of using these movements?

MOVE, FREEZE, PERFORM CHALLENGES

This routine for primary-grade children utilizes locomotor movements to develop aerobic capacity. Movement can be teacher or student directed with emphasis on combinations and variations of locomotor movements. Locomotor movements that should be presented are walking, running, skipping, galloping, sliding, hopping, jumping, and leaping. On signal, the class freezes and performs various challenges which might include the following:

1. Balance on one foot.
2. Do an animal walk (see following section).
3. Perform an exercise such as push-up, sit-up, or arm circles.
4. Perform a stretching activity (see page 84).
5. Move and write your name on the floor in giant letters.
6. Perform a partner stunt such as leapfrog or wring the dishrag.
7. Perform a stunt. For example, jump and do a heel click, or leap and clap the hands overhead.

8. Ask students to create their own challenge and demonstrate it to a friend.

The tasks should be simple and easy to perform. They should not require much instruction or the pace of the routine will be slowed. Try to include a balance of activities that assure development of the arm and shoulder girdle and abdominal regions.

ANIMAL MOVEMENTS

Animal movements are excellent fitness activities because they develop both cardiovascular endurance and strength. They are particularly enjoyable for primary-grade children because they can mimic the sounds and movements of the animals. Most of the animal movements are done with the body weight on all four limbs. This assures that the upper body receives attention to stimulate muscular development. Children can be challenged to move randomly throughout the area, across the gymnasium, or between cones delineating a specific distance. The distance to move can be increased or the amount of time each walk is done can be raised in order to assure that overload occurs. Following are examples of animal walks that can be used. Many more can be created simply by asking students to see "if they can move like a specific animal."

- *Puppy walk*—move on all fours (not the knees). Keep the head up and move lightly.
- *Lion walk*—move on all fours while keeping the back arched. Move deliberately and lift the "paws" to simulate moving without sound.
- *Elephant walk*—move heavily throughout the area, swinging the head back and forth like the elephant's trunk.
- *Seal walk*—move using the arms to propel the body. The legs are allowed to drag along the floor much as a seal would move.
- *Injured coyote walk*—move using only three limbs. Hold the injured limb off the floor. Vary the walk by specifying which limb is injured.
- *Crab walk*—move on all fours with the tummy facing the ceiling. Try to keep the back as straight as possible.
- *Rabbit walk*—start in a squatting position with the hands on the floor. Reach forward with the hands and support the body weight. Jump both feet toward the hands. Repeat the sequence.

After youngsters have learned a number of animal movements, they can be challenged to develop new ideas. In addition, stretching and flexibility activities should be alternated with the animal walks.

- *Variation:* An enjoyable fitness activity for children is playing "shark." In this game, youngsters perform their animal walks and flexibility activities in regular fashion. However, whenever the teacher shouts "Shark! Shark!" the class stops whatever they are doing and quickly runs throughout the area while making swimming movements with the arms. When the teacher tells the class that "everybody is safe now," the class resumes the animal walks.

FOUR CORNERS FITNESS

Arrange a number of cones so they outline a large rectangle. At each corner, place a small poster that lists a number of movement activities. Students are spread out around the perimeter of the rectangle and move in a clockwise direction. As they pass each cone, they perform one of the listed movement activities. The movement is continuous until the teacher gives a signal to "freeze." The signal indicates that it is time to perform a stretching or strength development activity that allows youngsters to recover from the aerobic activity.

When the stationary activity is completed, youngsters resume moving around the perimeter.

Following are examples of activities that can be used for movement around the perimeter: running, skipping, leaping, hopping, jumping, sliding, various animal walks, rope-jumping, moving over and around obstacles such as cones and benches, and rolling a hoop or ball while moving. To vary the aerobic demand placed on the youngsters, increase or decrease the size of the rectangle.

FITNESS GAMES   Fitness games are excellent for cardiovascular endurance and create a high degree of motivation. Emphasis should be placed on *all* students moving. One of the best ways to assure that this occurs is to play games that do not eliminate players. This usually means that players who tag someone are no longer "it" and the person tagged becomes "it." This also makes it difficult for players to tell who is "it," which is desirable since it assures that players cannot stop and stand when the "it" player is a significant distance from them. If various games stipulate a "safe" position, allow that the player can only remain in this position for a maximum of 5 seconds. This will assure that activity continues. Following are examples of games that can be played:

- *Stoop tag*—players cannot be tagged when they stoop.
- *Back-to-back tag*—players are safe when they stand back to back with another player. Other positions can be designated such as toe to toe, knee to knee, etc.
- *Train tag*—form groups of three or four and make a train by holding the hips of the other players. Three or four players are designated as "it" and try to hook onto the rear of the train. If "it" is successful, the player at the front of the train becomes the new "it."
- *Color tag*—players are safe when they stand on a specified color. The "safe" color may be changed by the leader at any time.
- *Elbow swing tag*—players cannot be tagged as long as they are performing an elbow swing with another player.
- *Balance tag*—players are safe when they balance on one body part.
- *Push-up tag*—players are safe when they are in push-up position. Other exercise positions such as sit-up, V-up, and crab position can be used.
- *Spider tag*—players are in groups of four with their backs toward each other and elbows joined. Two or more groups of "spiders" are designated as it. If the group breaks apart while being chased, they become "it."
- *Group tag*—the only time players are safe is when they are in a group (stipulated by the leader) holding hands. For example, the number might be "4" which means that students must be holding hands in groups of four to be safe.

OBSTACLE COURSE   This approach makes use of a youngster's natural urge to overcome obstacles, which involves going around, climbing, or moving under. Many commercial courses are made for the playground. These consist of parallel bars, tunnels, balance beams, monkey bars, chinning bars, figure eight poles, and walls to climb. The drawback of these courses is that they never change and, thus, their initial novelty to youngsters decreases over time. Another problem lies in the fact that many cannot be used in inclement weather.

Many homemade courses can be put together using equipment and apparatus commonly found in most physical education programs. Following is an example of a course that might be developed:

1. Figure eight run. Set out three to six cones spaced 5 yards apart. Students weave in and out of the cones.
2. Move over five hurdles. For primary-grade children, broomsticks laid across cones make excellent hurdles.
3. Crab walk from one cone to the next.
4. Do the agility run five times between two cones.
5. Go through a tunnel formed by a tumbling mat set on four chairs. Use more than one mat to make the tunnel longer.
6. Climb to the top of a rope or hang for 20 seconds.
7. Move through six hoops held in position with carpet squares.
8. Leap over five carpet squares.

TEACHING HINT

When starting youngsters in various circuits, spread them out over the distance of the course. This avoids having a large group of students standing in line, but it also prevents students from having to perform in front of other students who are waiting for their turn. Students who are faster can then pass others without slower youngsters feeling the stigma of being last.

PARACHUTE

The parachute has been a popular item in elementary physical education for many years. Usually used to promote teamwork, provide maximum participation, stimulate interest, or play games, the parachute perhaps has been overlooked as a tool to develop physical fitness. By combining vigorous shaking movement, circular movement, and selected exercises while holding onto the chute, exciting fitness routines can be developed.

Instructional Procedures

1. The parachute should be held at the waist during instructional episodes.
2. Each exercise or movement should be started and stopped with a signal (i.e., "Ready, Go!" and "Ready, Stop!")
3. Background music or the tom-tom provide motivating rhythmical accompaniment.
4. Children should be spaced evenly around the parachute.
5. Functional rest periods (stretching activities) should be interspersed throughout the vigorous activity.

Routine

1. Jog in a circular manner, holding the chute in the left hand.
2. Stop. Grip the chute with two hands and make small and/or big waves.
3. Slide to the right for 16 counts. Repeat to the left for 16 counts.
4. Stop. Lie on back, legs under chute with knees flexed and feet flat on the floor. Pull the chute to the chin until it becomes taut. Perform sit-up exercise (12 to 16 repetitions) while holding onto the chute with both hands.
5. Hold chute with overhand grip and skip (20 to 30 seconds).
6. Stop. Face the center of the chute, spread legs slightly, and flex knees slightly. Pull chute down toward legs. Hold for 5 to 10 seconds. Repeat three to six times.
7. Run in place while holding the chute at different levels. Continue for 20 to 30 seconds.
8. Sit with legs extended under the chute and arms extended forward holding the chute taut. Using only the muscles of the buttocks, move to

the center of the chute. Return to the original position. Repeat the sequence four to eight times.

9. Set the chute on the ground. Ask children to jog away from the chute and, on signal (whistle, drum, etc.), return to chute at same pace (30 seconds).

10. Facing away from the chute and using an overhand grip, hold the chute above the head with arms extended and pull as hard as possible without losing balance. Hold the position for 3 to 5 seconds. Repeat four to six times.

11. Jump up and down as quickly as possible while shaking the chute (15 to 20 seconds).

12. Make a dome by lifting the chute above the head and bringing it to the floor. Holding the edge of the chute down with both hands, do as many push-ups as possible before the center of the chute touches the floor.

13. Hop to the right for eight counts, then to the left for eight counts. Repeat three to five times.

14. Face the center and pull hard (tug-o-war) for 5 to 10 seconds. Repeat three to five times.

15. Conclude by making a dome and having everyone move inside the chute and sit on the rim with the back supporting the dome. Rotate trunk to the left for 10 seconds, then to the right for 10 seconds.

JOGGING   Jogging can be an excellent activity for developing fitness in youngsters when it is presented correctly. A large share of the experiences youngsters have had with jogging involved running laps as fast as possible in order to "win the race." The fastest youngsters receive the praises of teacher and peers while the slow (and often obese) youngster is chided for being so slow. It is mandatory for students to learn that when you run for your health, it is not a race.

Allow youngsters to find a friend of equal ability and randomly jog/walk throughout the playground area. Using a timer, begin with 4 minutes of continuous movement alternated with a rest period of 2 minutes where stretching exercises are performed. A final bout of 4 minutes of movement can complete the fitness workout.

An alternate method is to jog/walk for 2 minutes, stop and stretch for 1, move 2, stretch 1, move 2, and finish with 1 or 2 minutes of cool-down stretching and walking. Students can freeze on signal wherever they are and follow the teacher. Another alternative is have each partner lead a couple of stretching activities. Whatever method is used, make sure emphasis is placed on the joy of moving.

TEACHING HINT

When youngsters are allowed to find a friend to jog or exercise with, they usually will find someone of similar ability. This automatically gears the activity to their fitness and ability level. It also assures that the activity will be socially enjoyable and meaningful for the students. Most adults like to exercise with others and it is not unrealistic to expect that children like to exercise with friends.

Students should run in any direction, with a friend, and be able to visit while jogging. Ask students to jog for a specified amount of time rather than distance. This will allow them to individualize the amount of jogging they do based upon their ability and condition. The positive experience of running with a friend makes jogging a rewarding activity.

Following are some suggestions that might help increase youngsters' level of motivation to jog. All of them are designed to improve physical conditioning and to increase the amount of knowledge gained from the experience:

1. Set up a number of exercise trails on the playground. Trails should be of differing lengths so students can increase their workload as their fitness levels improve. Encourage them to keep track of their "mileage" by recording it on a class chart.

2. Jog across the USA by posting a map of the country in the classroom. Each day, the mileage of each student is added together and the distance plotted on the map. This tends to bring the class together for a common cause and all can feel as though they are making a meaningful contribution.

3. Set up a large clock in the playground area with a highly visible second hand so students can learn to monitor their heart rates. Encourage them to maintain the heart rate in the target zone for 5 to 10 minutes prior to participation in recess activities. When students are involved in activities that demand longer bouts of activity, i.e., soccer, team handball, and tag games, have them stop periodically and monitor their heart rates.

4. Develop a jogging course that utilizes playground equipment for strength development. Most playgrounds have chin-up bars, monkey bars, climbing equipment, and parallel bars. Organize a red, white, and blue circuit whereby each color indicates a greater workload. Develop the circuit so youngsters have to jog between each strength development station.

5. Develop an afterschool jogging and/or fitness club. A great deal of time and energy is spent on developing sport programs for children even though it is well documented that a large majority of students do not possess the genetic traits to be outstanding athletes. This is the attractiveness of a fitness club; every student, regardless of genetic talent, can improve his or her level of physical fitness. The club should focus on fitness gains and teach a large number of aerobic activities besides jogging, i.e., bicycling, hiking, power walking, cross-country running, and rope-jumping. Students can learn to get fit in order to play sports, which contrasts with the typical pattern of playing sports with the hope (usually unrealized) of developing physical fitness.

INTERVAL TRAINING

Interval training is an excellent activity for young children since they recover quickly from fatigue. Interval training involves controlling the work and rest intervals of the participants. Intervals of work (large muscle movement dominated by locomotor movements) and rest (dominated by nonlocomotor activity or walking) can be measured in time. Other ways of measuring intervals is to count repetitions or distance covered. The most practical method to use with elementary school children is to time the alternated work and rest periods.

Interval training can also be done by monitoring the heart rate. The work interval continues until the heart rate reaches the target zone and then the rest interval continues until the heart rate returns to approximately 120 to 140 beats per minute. The simplest example would be to alternate jogging and walking episodes. However, with elementary school children, this can be quite boring. Following are examples of some activities that can be alternated with rest activities:

High fives: Youngsters run around the area and, on signal, run to a partner, jump, and give a "high five." Various locomotor movements can be used as well as different styles of the "high five."

Over and under: Students find a partner. One partner makes a bridge on the floor while the other moves over, under, and around the bridge. This continues until a signal is given to "switch," which notifies them to change positions. This automatically assures that one child will be moving (working) while the other is resting. Try different types of bridges and movements to offer variety to the activity.

Rope jump and stretch: Each student has a jump rope and is jumping during the work interval. On signal, the student performs a stretch using the jump rope. An example would be to fold the rope in half and hold it overhead while stretching from side to side and to the toes.

Glue and stretch: Working with a partner, one partner is "it" and tries to stick like glue to the other. Students should move athletically, under control. The person who is not "it" tries to elude the other. On signal, "it" leads the other person in a stretching (resting) activity. On the next signal, the roles are reversed.

Rubber band: Students move throughout the area. On signal, they time a move to the center of the area. Upon reaching the center simultaneously, they jump upward and let out a loud "yea!" or similar exhortation and resume running throughout the area. The key to the activity is to synchronize the move to the center. After a number of runs, take a rest and stretch, or walk.

These are examples of movements and activities that can be done with interval training. A valuable addition to the activities is music. An effective approach is to prepare a tape recording of popular music. To begin, tape 30 seconds of music followed by 20 seconds of rest. Continue taping a number of these alternating music and silent intervals. The music sequence will direct youngsters to perform the work interval while the silence will signal that it is time to stretch or walk. This frees the teacher to help youngsters who are in need and assures that the intervals are timed accurately. As the youngsters become more fit, the length of the music bouts can be increased by making a new recording. Changing the music on a regular basis keeps children motivated.

INTERVAL TRAINING UTILIZING SHUTTLE MOVEMENTS

Shuttle movements are often used as a competitive activity for the purpose of declaring a winning team. However, a better use of shuttle movements is to enhance fitness since they alternate rest and strenuous movement intervals. The workload can be added to increasing the distance shuttle team members are asked to move and by decreasing the size of the teams. The shuttle movements are performed for a certain amount of time rather than a specified number of repetitions.

Students should be rotated into different teams on a regular basis so competition is minimized. Try to limit teams to less than five members so the rest interval is short. Use simple locomotor movements that all class members can perform so the activities are success oriented. Include a variety of locomotor movements to increase the novelty and challenge of the activity. Complex motor skills such as dribbling, passing, and shooting baskets should be avoided since they slow the pace and negate the aerobic value of the activities. Clearly mark the starting and returning points with cones.

Following are examples of shuttle movements that can be used to enhance aerobic fitness:

1. *Potato shuttle.* Three hoops are placed an equal distant apart in the running lanes in front of each team as shown in Figure 5–1. Beanbags or similar objects can be used as "potatoes" which are located in a fourth hoop immediately in front of each team. On signal, the first person places one beanbag in each of the hoops. Only one beanbag can be moved at a time. The next person in line picks up the beanbags from the hoops (one at a time) and deposits them in front of the next person waiting for a turn.

2. *Tag and go.* Half of the team members are placed at the end of the area opposite the remaining students. On signal, one team member runs to the other end of the area and tags a team member who continues back in the opposite direction. The tagging and shuttling back and forth continues until students are signaled to stop.

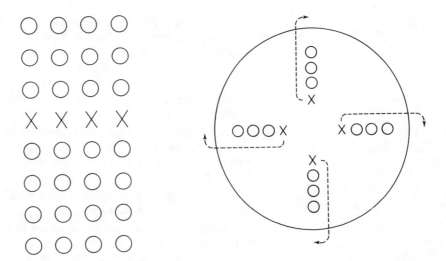

Figure 5-1 Potato Shuttle   **Figure 5-2** Around the Wheel

3. *Spider shuttle.* Students get back to back with a team member and hook elbows. On signal, they move to the turning point and return.

4. *Through the tunnel.* Make a tunnel in front of each team using benches with a mat placed over them. If this equipment is not available, use a number of hoops held up with carpet squares. On signal, students move forward, go through the tunnel, move to the turning point, and return.

5. *Rescue relay.* The first team member moves to the turning point and returns to pick up (rescue) the next player. These two players hold hands, run to the turning point, and return to pick up the next player. The activity continues until the complete team runs to the turning point and returns. At that point, the last person to be picked up becomes the new rescuer and the process repeats itself.

6. *Around the wheel.* Team members are aligned inside the wheel facing the center as shown in Figure 5-2. Use a number of cones to outline the circle. The first player in line is given a baton to carry. On signal, the first player in each squad moves clockwise around the outside of the wheel and returns to the inside of the circle at the end of the line. The baton is passed forward to the player at the front of the line who now runs around the wheel. Repeat until signaled to stop.

FITNESS ACTIVITIES WITH PARTNERS

Partner activities are an enjoyable fitness activity for intermediate-grade youngsters. They can be used to develop aerobic endurance, strength, and flexibility. Another advantage of partner fitness activities is that they can be performed indoors as a rainy day activity.

It is best if youngsters are paired with someone of similar size. In addition, telling youngsters to pair up with a friend will help assure they have found a partner who is caring and understanding. Emphasis should be placed on continuous movement and activity. Following are examples of challenging and enjoyable partner activities:

1. *Circle five.* Partner 1 stands stationary in the center of the circle with one palm up. Partner 2 runs in a circle around partner 1 and "gives him or her five" when passing the upturned palm.

2. *Foot tag.* Partners stand facing each other. On signal, they try to touch each other's toes with their feet. Emphasize the importance of a touch as opposed to a stamp or kick.

3. *Knee tag.* Partners stand facing each other. On signal, they try to tag the other person's knees. Each time a tag is made, a point is scored. Play for a designated amount of time.

4. *Mini Merry-Go-Round.* Partners face each other with their feet nearly touching and their hands grasped in a double wrist grip. Partners slowly lean backward while keeping their feet in place until their arms are straight. Then they spin around as quickly as possible. It is important that partners be of similar size.

5. *Around and under.* One partner stands with feet spread shoulder width apart and one hand in front of the body with the palm up. The other partner goes between the standing partner's legs, stands up, and slaps the partner's hand. Continue the pattern for a designated time.

6. *Ball wrestle.* Both partners grasp an 8 1/2-inch playground ball and try to wrestle it away from each other.

7. *Sitting wrestle.* Partners sit on the floor facing each other with legs bent, feet flat on the floor, toes touching, and hands grasped. The goal of the activity is to pull the other's buttocks off the floor.

8. *Upset the alligator.* One partner lays face down on the floor. On signal, the other partner tries to turn the alligator over. The alligator tries to avoid being turned on his or her back.

9. *Seat balance wrestle.* Partners sit on the floor facing each other with their knees raised and feet off the floor. If desired, they can place the hands under the thighs to help support the legs. They start with the toes touching and try to tip each other backward using their toes.

10. *Head wrestle.* One partner holds the other's left wrist with the right hand. On signal, he or she tries to touch the partner's head with his or her left hand. Repeat and try to touch with the opposite hand.

11. *Pull apart.* One partner stands with feet spread, arms bent at the elbows in front of the chest, with the fingertips touching. Partner 2 holds the wrists of the other and tries to pull the fingertips apart. Jerking is not allowed; the pull must be smooth and controlled.

12. *Pin dance.* Partners hold hands facing each other with a bowling pin (or cone) placed between them. On signal, they try to cause each other to touch the pin.

13. *Finger fencing.* Partners face each other with their feet in front of each other in a straight line. The toes on the front foot of each partner should touch. Partners lock index fingers and attempt to cause each other to move either foot from the beginning position.

Exercises for Developing Fitness Routines

Selection and incorporation of exercises into the fitness module should be based on the fitness, abilities, and interest of children and the potential for the exercise to contribute to total body development. To be effective, fitness routines must be comprised of various exercises that develop components of skill- and health-related physical fitness. Exercises, in themselves, are not sufficient to develop cardiovascular endurance. Additional exercise, in the form of aerobic activity, is needed to round out fitness development.

There are innumerable exercises that effectively place demands on the muscles of the arm and shoulder girdle, lower back, leg, and abdominal area. Some exercises and exercise practices, however, pose inherent hazards to long-term musculoskeletal growth and development as well as possible injury, thus dictating avoidance. Cautious selection of exercises, based on sound principles, is a better approach to fitness than an overzealous attempt that may place unnecessary exercise demands on the child. Usually, any potentially harmful exercise activity can be prevented through knowledgeable instructors, proper technique, and careful adherence to the guidelines for fitness development discussed in Chapter 2.

EXERCISES TO AVOID   Following are examples of potentially harmful exercises or practices that should be avoided when selecting fitness activities for children:

1. Straight-legged sit-ups place unnecessary demands on the muscles of the lower back which may cause excessive lower back curve. The sit-up and its many variations should be performed with the knees bent and feet placed about 15 inches from the buttocks. The curling up movement should be smooth and controlled with the chin tucked to the chest. This not only makes for a safe exercise, it also assures proper isolation of the abdominal muscles.

2. Ballistic (forceful bouncing) stretching activities should be avoided. Static (slow) stretching, which applies smooth and constant pressure on muscle groups, is effective in improving flexibility and is considerably safer. Children should be encouraged to stretch to the point of pull, allow the muscles to relax naturally, and then stretch further. Control, slow and sustained, is the watchword for proper stretching technique.

3. Exercises that cause hyperextension of the neck can cause pinching of the arteries and nerves at the base of the skull and should be avoided. Activities such as inverted bicycle, wrestler's bridge, and neck arching, which place undue pressure on the neck, should also be excluded. Comfortable rotation of the neck is recommended as a safe exercise for neck muscle development.

4. Full squats, or deep knee bends, may cause damage to the growth and development of the knee joints and should be avoided. Exercises that extend the knee to 90 degrees are effective for proper development of the knee joint.

5. Stretching activities done from a standing position can cause children to hyperextend the knee, excessively stretching ligaments. Youngsters should be allowed to relax, even flex, the knee joint during standing stretches. A general rule of thumb is to have children judge their own range of motion.

6. Exercises that cause hyperextension in the lower back should be avoided. Specific examples of contraindicated exercises are back bends, straight-leg raises from a supine position, straight-legged sit-ups, and prone back arch. There are much better ways to exercise the back than arching.

CATEGORIES OF EXERCISES   Selected exercises are grouped into categories based on their contribution to fitness in the following areas: (1) arm and shoulder girdle, (2) flexibility, (3) leg, and (4) trunk and abdominal. From 6 to 12 exercises should be included in any one fitness routine. Each routine should include two exercises from each of the four groups plus sufficient aerobic activity to elevate the heart rate into the training zone. It is recommended that exercises, as well as fitness routines, be changed on a regular basis.

Recommended exercises are presented under each of the four major categories. The starting position, movement and counting sequence, and variations are listed with each exercise.

Exercises for the Arm and Shoulder Girdle Region   Arm and shoulder girdle exercises in this section include free-arm, arm-support, or partner-assisted types.

Arm Circles

Starting position. Stand erect, with feet about shoulder width apart and arms straight and extended to the side.

Movement. Rotating from the shoulders, simultaneously circle arms forward or backward.

Variations. (1) With palms up or down, make small, medium, and large circles. (2) Circle the arms in alternate directions.

Crab Kick

Starting position. The body is supported by the hands and feet, with the back parallel to the floor. The knees should be bent at right angles and the buttocks clearly off the floor.

Movement. Kick the right leg up and down (counts 1 and 2). Repeat with left leg (counts 3 and 4) as shown in Figure 5–3.

Variations. In the crab position: (1) Extend the right leg so it rests on the floor (count 1). Return the right leg to the starting position while extending the left leg (count 2). (2) Extend both legs forward (count 1). Return to starting position (count 2). (3) Move forward, backward, sideways, and in various patterns. (4) Lift the right arm so it points to the ceiling and return it to its original weight-bearing position (counts 1 and 2). Repeat with left arm (counts 3 and 4).

Partner Pull-ups

Starting position: One partner stands erect, with feet spread slightly more than shoulder width apart and arms extended toward the floor. The other child lies on his or her back between the feet of the person standing and grasps the partner's hands (Figure 5–4).

Figure 5-3 Variation of the Crab Kick

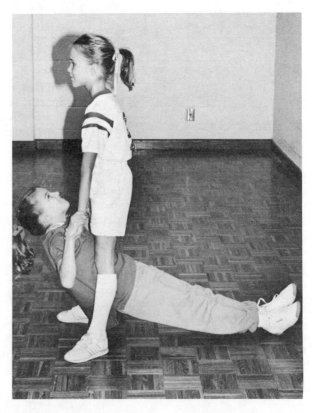

Figure 5-4 Partner Pull-Up

Figure 5-5 Inclined Wall Push-Up

Movement: Keeping the body rigid and using only the arms, the partner on the floor pulls his or her body approximately 12 to 18 inches off the floor (count 1) and returns to starting position (count 2).

Variations: Use different hand grips (i.e., hands grasp wrists, shake hands, interlock fingers, etc.)

Inclined Wall Push-Ups (Figure 5-5)

Starting position: This exercise can be done with either the feet or the hands on the wall. The hands version is easier and should precede the push-up with feet on the wall. In the hands version, the hands are placed on the wall while the feet walk as far from the wall as possible. The farther the performer's feet move from the wall, the more inclined and difficult the push-up will be.

Movement: The elbows are bent as the body is slowly moved toward the wall. Using only the arms, the body is returned to the starting position.

Push-Ups

Starting position: Assume a front-leaning rest position, with body straight and hands flat on the floor. Fingers should point forward.

Movement: Bending from the elbows, slowly lower the body until the chest touches the floor (count 1). Using only the arms, return to starting position (count 2).

Variations: (1) Change the movement sequence. For example, halfway down (count 1), to the floor (count 2), halfway up (count 3), to starting position (count 4). (2) Alter the starting position. Children who have difficulty supporting their weight may be successful if the push-up sequence is completed while resting part of their body weight on the knees. (3) Varying the hand position can make the exercise more challenging.

Pull-Ups

Starting position: Hang from a horizontal bar. Feet should not touch the floor.

Movement: Keeping the body straight, use only the arms to pull the body up until the chin is above the bar (count 1). Return to starting position (count 2).

Variations: (1) Hang from a low bar, heels on the floor, with body straight from feet to head. Lower the body to the floor (count 1). Pull up, keeping the body straight, until the chest touches the bar (count 2). (2) Change the hand grip (i.e., palms forward, palms away, or one hand).

Exercises to Increase Flexibility   Numerous exercises develop and maintain flexibility. Those included in this section specifically exercise the muscles of the lower back and posterior thigh. Students need to be instructed and continually reminded that, to decrease the possibility of muscle injury, all stretching exercises should be done slowly (static stretching). While flexibility exercises are specific and important to total fitness development, they also can serve as functional rest periods during vigorous fitness activities and should be interspersed throughout exercise routines accordingly.

Lower Leg Stretch (Figure 5-6)

Starting position: Stand facing a wall with the feet about shoulder width apart. Place the palms of the hands on the wall at eye level.

Movement: Walk away from the wall, keeping the body straight, until the stretch is felt in the lower portion of the calf. The feet should remain flat on the floor during the stretch.

Leg Pick-Up (Figure 5-7)

Starting position: Sit on the floor with the legs spread. Reach forward and grab the outside of the ankle with one hand and the outside of the knee with the other.

Movement: Pick the leg up and pull the ankle toward the chin. The back of the upper leg should be stretched. Repeat the stretch, lifting the other leg.

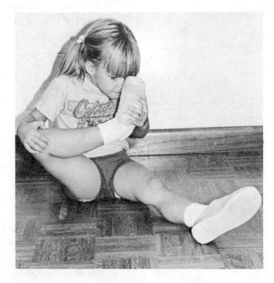

Figure 5-6 Lower Leg Stretch   **Figure 5-7** Leg Pick-Up

Bend and Stretch

Starting position: Stand erect with feet slightly more than shoulder width apart and arms extended above the head.

Movement: Gradually bend forward for seven counts trying to touch the floor between the feet. Flex knees if necessary. Return to starting position on the eighth count.

Variations: (1) Bend sideways or backward. (2) Change leg positions (legs together, cross legs, or spread legs farther apart).

Knee-to-Chest Curl

Starting position: Lie on the back in a curled position with forearms behind knees and face tucked into knees.

Movement: Pull knees to chest and curl the pelvis off the floor. Hold in stretched (curled) position for 15 to 20 seconds. Return to starting position.

Variations: In curled position, rock back and forth or side to side on the lower back.

Sitting Stretch

Starting position: Sit on the floor with legs spread and extended. Arms are extended above the head with one hand on top of the other.

Movement: Bend from the hips and reach forward slowly for seven counts holding the seventh count at the farthest point reached. Return to the starting position on the eighth count.

Variations: Bend to the left on the first count and gradually move to the right for the seventh count. Return to the starting position on the eighth count.

Feet Together Stretch

Starting position: Sit with the knees bent and the soles of the feet touching (Figure 5–8). Reach forward with the hands and grasp the toes.

Figure 5–8 Feet Together Stretch

Figure 5-9 Leg Hug (Phase 1)

Figure 5-10 Leg Hug (Phase 2)

Movement: Gently pull on the toes and bend forward from the hips, applying stretch to the inside of the legs and lower back. To increase the stretching effect, place the elbows on or near the knees and press them toward the floor.

Leg Hug

Starting position: Lie on the back with feet flat on the floor, knees flexed, and head resting on the floor. Arms should be parallel to the torso and resting on the floor (Figure 5-9).

Movement: Arch back and lift hips approximately 6 to 8 inches off the floor and hold for several counts (Figure 5-10). Relax and use hands to pull knees to chest and hold for several counts.

Variations: (1) Alternate legs during the pulling phase of this exercise. (2) Fold arms on the chest. Lift the hips off the ground, holding for several counts. Return to starting position.

Squat Stretch (Figure 5-11)

Starting position: Begin in a standing position with the legs shoulder width apart and the feet pointed outward.

Figure 5-11 Squat Stretch

Figure 5-12 Standing Hip Bend

Figure 5-13 Sit and Twist

Movement: Gradually move to a squatting position, keeping the feet flat on the floor if possible. If balance is a problem, the stretch can be done while leaning against a wall.

Standing Hip Bend (Figure 5-12)

Starting position: Stand with one hand on the hip and the other arm overhead.

Movement: Bend to the side with the hand resting on the hip. The arm overhead should point and move in the direction of the stretch with a slight bend at the elbow. Reverse and stretch the opposite side.

Sit and Twist

Starting position: Sit on floor with legs crossed, trunk erect, and eyes looking straight ahead. Arms should be relaxed and in front of body (Figure 5-13).

Movement: Place the right hand on the outside of the left thigh and pull while twisting the body to the left. Hold for several counts. Return to starting position. Repeat on the opposite side of the body.

Variations: Place a beanbag or other object behind the student and see if he or she can reach it by slowly twisting from the trunk.

Hip Circles

Starting position: Stand with legs partially bent and feet shoulder width apart. Clasp the hands in front of the body with the arms straight and held near the knees.

Movement: Slowly make large circles with the hands by bending at the joints including the ankles, knees, hips, and shoulders. Make circles in both directions. The knees should remain flexed throughout the entire activity.

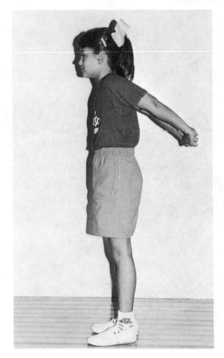

Figure 5-14 Wishbone Stretch   **Figure 5-15** Calf Bends

Wishbone Stretch (Figure 5-14)

Starting position: Move the arms behind the back and clasp hands.

Movement: Keep the arms straight and raise the hands toward the ceiling to stretch the shoulder girdle.

Variation: Stand near a wall (back toward the wall) and place the hands on it. Gently bend at the knees and lower the body while keeping the hands at the same level.

Calf Bends

Starting position: Stand with the hands on the hips and the feet in a forward stride position (widely spread with one foot in front of the body and the other to the rear). Point the toes forward (Figure 5–15).

Movement: Slowly bend the front leg as far as possible, stretching the calf of the back leg. Be sure to keep the heels on the ground. Hold the position for 5 seconds; reverse the positioning of the feet and stretch the other calf.

Exercises for the Leg Region   All locomotor movements and other types of physical activity (i.e., rope-jumping, cycling, etc.) can be used to develop leg strength and endurance. In addition to developing muscular strength and endurance, most leg exercises also improve agility. Exercises in this section are designed for use in structured fitness routines and have potential aerobic benefits.

Treadmill

Starting position: Assume a push-up position with one leg brought forward so the knee is under the chest (Figure 5–16).

Movement: Reverse the position of the knees, bringing the extended knee forward (count 1). Return to the original position (count 2).

Figure 5-16 Treadmill

Variations: Change the cadence of the exercise (slow to fast).

Run in Place

Starting position: Stand erect.

Movement: Alternate bringing the knees up in front of the body. Be sure the arms are in the correct position for running.

Variations: (1) Extend arms to the side, forward, and above the head (Figure 5-17) (2) Bring heels up behind the body when running. (3) Run in small circles, making a figure eight and other patterns. (4) Change tempo.

Jumping Jacks

Starting position: Stand at attention.

Figure 5-17 Variation of Running in Place

Figure 5-18 Variation of the Jumping Jack

Movement: Jump to a straddle position with the arms above the head (count 1). Return to starting position (count 2).

Variations: (1) From a forward stride position, move feet forward and backward (Figure 5–18). (2) Rotate the body in a circular manner while performing the jumping jack. (3) Cross the feet on the return move (count 2). (4) Alternate kicking the leg up and forward on count 1. (5) Change the movement of the hands on count 1.

Stride Jump

Starting position: Stand with one leg forward and the other back, with the knees bent in a half-squat position. Hands are clasped behind neck with elbows pointing to the side.

Movement: Jump straight up and reverse the positions of the legs (count 1). Return to starting position (count 2).

Variations: (1) Move sideways, forward, or backward while performing the exercise. (2) Hold arms to the side or above the head. (3) Move arms forward and backward in opposition to leg movement.

Power Jumper

Starting position: Crouched, with knees flexed and arms extended backward.

Movement: Jump as high as possible and extend arms upward and over the head.

Variations: (1) Jump and turn. (2) Change the number of repetitions to be completed during a certain time period. (3) Jump and perform a task (i.e., heel click, clap hands, imagine catching a thrown pass or snaring a rebound).

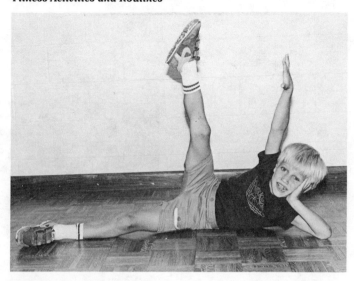

Figure 5–19 Side Leg Flex

Side Leg Flex (Figure 5-9)

Starting position: Lie on the floor on one side of the body. Rest the head in the right hand and place the left hand along the side of the body.

Movement: On the first count, lift the left leg and arm and point them toward the ceiling. Return to the starting position on the second count. Rotate to the other side of the body after performing the desired number of repetitions.

Variation: The double-side leg flex demands more effort. Both legs are lifted simultaneously as far off the floor as possible.

Front Leg Kick

Starting position: Begin in a forward standing position.

Movement: Alternately kick each leg forward and as high as possible. This exercise should be done rhythmically so that all movement occurs on the toes. When the leg is kicked upward, the arm on the same side should be moved forward in an attempt to touch the toe of the lifted leg.

Exercises for the Trunk and Abdominal Region

For most abdominal exercises, the child starts from a supine position (on back) on the floor or mat. Most movements begin with a curl-up, rolling the head up first followed by the shoulders. To ensure maximum activity for the abdominal muscles and to prevent the hip flexors from overexertion, the chin should always be in contact or near contact with the sternum (chest). Further, the bent-knee position places greater demand on the abdominal muscles. For the most part, exercises for the abdominal region also benefit functioning of the lower back. Movements for the trunk and abdominal region should be large, vigorous, and done throughout the full range of motion.

Partial Curl

Starting position: Supine, with knees flexed and feet flat on the floor. Arms are extended forward and off the floor.

Movement: Keeping the chin tucked to the chest, roll the shoulders forward as far as possible without lifting the lower back off the floor (hold for seven counts; Figure 5–20). Return to starting position (count 8)

Figure 5-20 Partial Curl

Sit-Up (AAHPERD Physical Best Test)

Starting position: Lie on back, with knees flexed and arms folded across the chest with hands on opposite shoulders. Chin tucked to chest and shoulders slightly off the floor.

Movement: Curl up until forearms touch thighs (count 1). Return to starting position (count 2).

Leg Extension

Starting position: Sit on the floor with legs extended and hands on hips.

Movement: Sliding the feet on the floor, bring heels as close to the seat as possible (count 1, Figure 5-21). Return to starting position (count 2, Figure 5-22).

Variations: The exercise can be made more challenging by changing arm positions (i.e., extended to the side, in front, and folded across the chest).

Rowing (Figure 5-23)

Starting position: This exercise starts with the student in a supine position with the arms above the head.

Figure 5-21 Leg Extension (Count 1)

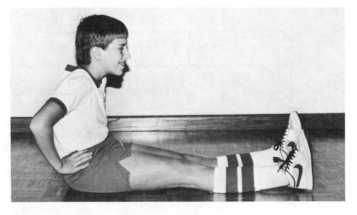

Figure 5-22 Leg Extension (Count 2)

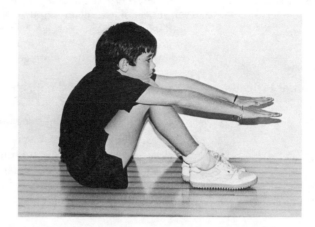

Figure 5-23 Rowing

Movement: This is a controlled two-count exercise. On the first count, the arms are moved toward the feet as the student moves to a sitting position; the knees are pulled simultaneously to the chest. On the second count, the student returns to starting position.

V-Seat

Starting position: Sitting on the floor. Arms are held parallel to the floor at shoulder height in front of the body.

Movement: Lean slightly back, lift the legs from the floor, and touch the feet with the fingertips. The body should form a "V." The V-seat can be repeated a set number of times or can be held for a set period of time.

Trunk Twister

Starting position: Stand erect with feet about shoulder width apart and hands on hips.

Movement: Bend downward (count 1). Rotating the trunk, bend to the right (count 2), bend backward (count 3), bend to the left (count 4). Return to the starting position.

Variation: Alternate direction of rotation.

Squat Thrust

Starting position: Standing at attention.

Movement: Drop to a squat position, with the hands flat on the floor, about shoulder width apart (count 1). Fully extend legs back, keeping them together (count 2). Pull legs to the squat position (count 3). Return to the starting position (count 4).

Variations: To place greater demands on the abdominal muscles, add an extra set of leg extensions and return to squat with each repetition.

Hip Walk

Starting position: Begin in sitting position with the legs straight and together.

Movement: Keep the abdominal muscles contracted while moving the buttocks forward by alternately "walking" the hips. Practice moving backward as well as forward.

TEACHER-LED EXERCISES There are certain advantages in having the teacher lead the class through a sequence of exercises. First, the teacher is able to display his or her own enthusiasm toward exercise. Second, the pace (intensity) of the activity can be controlled. Finally, by leading the exercises, the teacher creates a good opportunity to practice management skills.

Instructional Procedures

1. The teacher should change his or her location on the floor after each exercise.
2. The exercise cadence should be directed at the "norm" of the class.
3. Daily altering of the class formation (scatter, squad, circular, etc.) can add variety to the routine.
4. Providing a musical background will increase the children's motivation level.

Routine

Exercise	Repetitions or Time
Arm Circles	8–12 (8 forward, 8 backward) or 30 seconds
Bend and Stretch	8–12 or 30 seconds
Treadmill	12–15 (4 counts) or 25 seconds
Sit-Up	12–15 or 45 seconds
Single Leg Crab Kick	8–12 (2 left, 2 right) or 30 seconds
Knee to Chest Curl	3 (hold each curl for 15 seconds)
Run in Place	30 seconds
Trunk Twister	8–10 or 45 seconds

Conclude the routine with 2 to 4 minutes of jogging, rope-jumping, or other continuous activity.

STUDENT-LED EXERCISES There are times when students should be given an opportunity to lead either an exercise or the entire routine. To be effective in instructing their peers, student leaders should have had prior practice performing the exercise.

Instructional Procedures

1. The teacher should spend time before or after class instructing would-be leaders how to execute and count the exercise.
2. Provide leaders with laminated index cards explaining and graphically describing the exercise.
3. Predetermine the number of repetitions to be completed.
4. Ask for volunteers, or assign willing students to be leaders. No child should be forced into a position of leadership that could result in failure for both the youngster and the class.
5. The teacher should move freely among the class, helping those students who require additional assistance in performing the exercises successfully.

Routine

Exercise	Repetitions or Time
Push-Up	6–12 (2 counts) or 30 seconds
Sitting Stretch	8–12 or 45 seconds

Jumping Jacks	15–20 or 30 seconds
Leg Extension	10–15 or 45 seconds
Push-Up	6–8 (4 counts) or 40 seconds
Leg Hug	4–6 (hold counts 1 and 2 for 10 seconds)
Stride Jump	10–15 or 45 seconds
Squat Thrust	8–12 or 45 seconds

Conclude the routine with 2 to 4 minutes of jogging, rope-jumping, or other continuous activity.

EXERCISES TO MUSIC   Music adds a great deal of motivation to exercise activities for people of all ages. There are many commercial routines available that are somewhat motivating. The drawback lies in the fact that most of them are made for a specific group and, therefore, may be too easy or difficult for youngsters to perform. Another problem is that they cannot be changed, which makes it next to impossible to develop overload and progression.

The authors have had excellent success with making exercise tapes using a tape recorder and popular music. Depending on the sophistication of the equipment and the expertise of the teacher, excellent tapes can be made. Most media departments in schools have equipment that will allow music to be taped with vocal instructions dubbed onto the music track. The advantage of this approach is that the teacher can play the tape, which has commands for starting and stopping the exercises, moving around and helping students in need. Refer to the section on Teacher-Led Exercises for guidelines in developing a fitness routine that develops all body parts.

Another approach is to have students bring records and lead exercises based on their music. A group of students might work together to develop a routine as part of an out-of-class assignment.

Primary-grade exercises to music should focus on locomotor movements and various movement challenges. The use of music is an excellent beginning for developing the sense of moving to external rhythms.

TEACHING HINT

Taped music can be an excellent tool for timing the length of exercise bouts. For example, if doing Random Running, students could run/walk as long as the music is playing and stretch when it pauses. If the music is pretaped, it will free the teacher from having to keep an eye on a stopwatch. Other exercise modules that work well with music are circuit training, Grass Drills, Continuous Movement Routines, and Jump Rope Exercises.

AEROBIC DANCE   Aerobic dance is a popular fitness activity for children of all ages. It has the advantage of being demanding aerobic activity supported by upbeat music. For primary-grade children, the approach should be to develop activities that are rhythmic, yet uncomplicated. A common and highly effective approach is to use a "follow-the-leader" technique. The teacher can lead during the learning stages of the routine and gradually allow students to lead each other.

In developing routines for intermediate-grade children, movement changes are usually dictated by changes in the music. The most common pattern is to change every 8 or 16 beats. In order to make it easier for children to remember the sequences, activities can be listed on a large poster board. Routines often motivate more children when exact adherence to the routine is not demanded. Often, when everyone is expected to be exactly in the same place at the same time, it appears to students that precision rather than fitness is the goal. Remember that the primary goal is to develop a positive feeling toward activity, rather than developing a highly polished performance.

The activities should be appealing to both boys and girls. If the activities demand a great deal of rhythmic motor coordination, it is possible that boys will be turned off and see the activity as unimportant and feminine in nature. Large muscle activities that promote cardiovascular activity should form the basis of the routine. Once again, the teacher's enthusiasm can have an impact on the excitement and energy level of the class.

Suggested Activities   Following are examples of activities that can be used to create routines. In developing routines, start with a few simple activities such as running steps, and gradually increase the complexity of the activities.

Running and Walking Steps

- *Directional running steps*—forward, backward, diagonal, sideways, and turning.
- *Rhythmic runs*—run and do a specific movement on a specified beat. The first and fourth beats are the most commonly used and easiest to follow. Examples of movements that might be used are a knee lift, clap, hop, or jump turn.
- *Running variations*—lift the knees, lift and slap the knees, or kick up the heels.
- *Running with arms in various positions*—carry the arms in different positions such as on the hips, above the head, or extended at shoulder height. Run and clap the hands with arms extended at different levels and positions.

Exercises on the Floor

Many different exercises can be done rhythmically during a routine. It is important to use the exercises as a respite from the intense cardiovascular demands of the large muscle activity.

- *Sit-ups*—these can be modified and performed to two, four, or eight beats of the music. For example, a four count sit-up might be done as follows: (1) sit-up to knees, (2) touch the toes, (3) return to knees, and (4) return to the floor. V-ups can be held for four counts followed by a four-count rest.
- *Push-ups*—can be done to two or four counts. When doing four-count push-ups, the body is lowered and raised half the distance to the floor each count.
- *Side leg raises*—lie on the side and raise and lower the top leg to the beat of the music.
- *Crab kicking*—starting in the crab position, alternate extending one leg forward at a time. The rhythm should be similar to running in place.
- *Jumping jacks*—use different foot and hand positions and movements. For example, jump with the arms alternately extended upward and then pulled into the chest. Move the feet from side to side or forward and backward instead of the usual movement.

Bounce Steps

Bounce steps consist of jumping in place rhythmically. They are excellent beginning steps since they are not complex and encourage maintenance of an even rhythm.

- *Bounce and clap*—clapping can be done on every beat, every other beat, or every fourth beat.
- *Bounce, turn, and clap*—the body can be turned a quarter or half turn with each bounce.
- *Bounce and move*—the weight is transferred from side to side, forward and backward, or in a diagonal direction.
- *Bounce and twist*—extend the arms at shoulder level and twist the lower body back and forth on each bounce.
- *Bounce with floor patterns*—make various floor patterns with a specified number of bounces. For example, move in a circle, triangle, square, etc., using 16 bounces.
- *Bounce with kick variations*—perform different kicks such as knee lift, kick, knee lift and kick, double kicks, and knee lift and slap knees.

Using Equipment

A large variety of equipment can be used to enhance the experience for youngsters. Children really enjoy the opportunity to manipulate a jump rope, ball, hoop, or beanbag. The following are ideas that might be used:

- *Jump rope*—perform many of the basic steps such as forward, backward, slow, and fast time. Many of the steps described in the jump rope section can be used, depending on the skill of the students.
- *Hoop*—rhythmically swing the hoop around different body parts. Hula hoop using different body parts. Use the hoop as a jump rope and jump rhythmically.
- *Balls*—develop different routines by combining locomotor movements with bouncing, tossing, and dribbling skills.

CONTINUOUS MOVEMENT DRILLS The students are instructed to walk in a circular pattern, always maintaining a safe distance from their classmates. Throughout the routine, the teacher changes the locomotor movements, direction of movement, and frequently stops the class to perform selected exercises. Children of all ages enjoy being challenged by this fast-paced sequence of fitness activities and should derive aerobic benefits from the locomotor activities interspersed between exercises.

Instructional Procedures

1. To avoid singling out slower children, change the direction of the movement regularly. Children who continually lag behind can be moved toward the inner part of the circle. The faster children can pass them on the outside.
2. The teacher should be located inside the circle. This position allows ready access to students having difficulty with either the movements or exercises.
3. Use boundary cones or lines on the floor to mark the perimeter of the circle.

Routine

Exercises or Movements	Repetitions or Time
Jog	15–20 seconds
Double-leg Crab Kick	8–12 (4 counts) or 30 seconds
Skip	15–20 seconds
Sit and Twist	4–6 (5 seconds on each side)

Slide (clap when feet come together)	15–20 seconds
Jumping Jacks (variations)	10–15 (4 counts) or 30 seconds
Crab Walk (feet forward)	10–15 seconds
Sit-Up	8–12 or 45 seconds
Hop to the middle of the circle on the right foot.	
Hop to the original position on the left foot.	
Push-Up	6–12 or 40 seconds
Gallop	25–30 seconds
Leg Hug	3–6 (hold counts 1 and 2 for 10 seconds)
Walk. Reach arms to sides and perform arm circles.	
Power Jumper	8–12 or 30 seconds
Trot	15–20 seconds
Squat Thrust	6–10 or 40 seconds

For proper cool-down, conclude the routine with approximately 2 to 3 minutes of stretching.

CIRCUIT TRAINING   In circuit training, each of several (6–10) stations has designated exercises for a specified fitness component. Students are assigned to small groups and move from station to station, in a prescribed manner, completing the fitness tasks at each station. Each station should offer several exercises that place demands on the same muscle groups and vary in degree of difficulty. Figure 5–24 shows an example of an eight-station circuit.

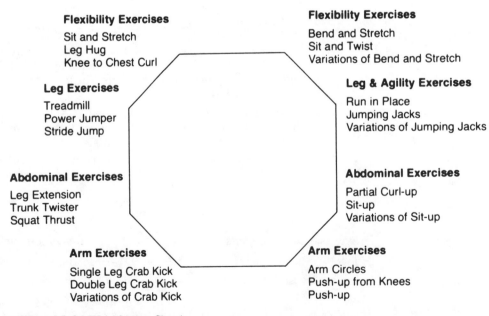

Flexibility Exercises

Sit and Stretch
Leg Hug
Knee to Chest Curl

Leg Exercises

Treadmill
Power Jumper
Stride Jump

Abdominal Exercises

Leg Extension
Trunk Twister
Squat Thrust

Arm Exercises

Single Leg Crab Kick
Double Leg Crab Kick
Variations of Crab Kick

Flexibility Exercises

Bend and Stretch
Sit and Twist
Variations of Bend and Stretch

Leg & Agility Exercises

Run in Place
Jumping Jacks
Variations of Jumping Jacks

Abdominal Exercises

Partial Curl-up
Sit-up
Variations of Sit-up

Arm Exercises

Arm Circles
Push-up from Knees
Push-up

Figure 5-24 Eight Station Circuit

Instructional Procedures

1. Exercises should be familiar to children and within their capabilities.

2. The exercises at each succeeding station should make demands on different parts of the body. This avoids undue fatigue and offers a greater variety in exercise.

3. The teacher should move around the area, assisting children who are having difficulty with certain exercises.

4. Children should be encouraged to correctly perform as many repetitions of the exercise as possible in the time allotted.

5. The movement from station to station should vary and offer cardiovascular benefits. Performing various locomotor movements around the entire circuit, passing the station just completed, and finishing in a ready position for the exercises at the next station is an example of a rotational movement. Animal walks also can be used to move from station to station.

6. There should be between four and six children at each station.

7. Equipment (i.e., jump ropes, playground balls, hula hoops, etc.) can add variety to the exercise station.

8. The exercise workload can be varied by increasing the time spent at each station. The recommended time at each station is 15 to 30 seconds.

9. Signals should be used to start the exercise interval and begin the rotation from station to station. Exercise tapes can be recorded to provide background music for the exercise bout and silent time for moving to the next station.

10. Stations that provide functional rest periods should be inserted following the more demanding exercises.

11. Colorful posters identifying and illustrating the exercises can be educational and motivational.

ROPE-JUMPING AND EXERCISE

Rope-jumping is an activity that has the potential for improving cardiovascular fitness, leg strength, and agility. A routine that alternates aerobic bouts of rope-jumping with exercises utilizing jump ropes to develop other components of physical fitness can be included in the daily physical education lesson.

Instructional Procedures

1. Children should be in extended squad or scatter formation. Each child should be a safe distance from the closest person.

2. Since children will incur greater fitness benefits if they are reasonably skilled at rope-jumping, this routine should be used only after the basic steps have been mastered.

3. Proper rope length can be measured by standing on the rope and holding the rope up the sides of the body. If the rope is the correct length, it should reach the armpits.

4. Cassette tapes can be recorded to signal the start and stop of the jumping and exercise segments, respectively.

5. The following exercises can be performed with jump ropes:

   Rope Jump Twist: Fold the rope and hold it overhead. Sway from side to side. Twist back and forth.

   Hamstring Stretch: Move to a supine position with the rope folded and held in outstretched hands pointing toward the ceiling. Bring up one leg at a time and touch the rope with the foot. Try bringing up both legs simultaneously.

Sitting Stretch: Begin in a sitting position with the legs extended. Fold the rope and try placing it over the soles of the feet. Move the rope overhead and twist the upper body in both directions.

Isometric Exercises: The following pulls should be performed using maximum force and held for 8 to 12 seconds: (1) Fold the rope and hold overhead. Pull as hard as possible. (2) Stand on the rope and attempt to pull it overhead. (3) Place the rope under the buttocks while standing in a semicrouched position. Pull both ends of the rope upward. (4) Fold the rope and place it under the feet. Bend over and grasp both ends. Pull on both ends of the rope by trying to stand up straight. (5) In a sitting position, place the folded rope over the feet. Pull the rope toward the buttocks. (6) Hold the ends of the rope horizontally in front of the body. Pull the ends away from the center of the body. (7) Place the folded rope behind the knees. Try to pull the rope forward. (8) Place the folded rope behind the back at shoulder level. Pull the ends of the rope forward.

Routine

Activity	*Repetitions or Time*
Basic Jumping (Forward Turning)	20–30 seconds
Rope Jump Twist	30 seconds
Basic Jumping (Backward Turning)	20–30 seconds
Partial Curl (8 counts)	6–10 repetitions or 45 seconds
Jump and Slowly Turn Body	20–30 seconds
Sitting Stretch	45 seconds
Hop on One Foot (Forward Turning)	10–15 seconds
Change Foot (Forward Turning)	10–15 seconds
Hamstring Stretch	30 seconds
Rocker Step	20–30 seconds
Isometric Exercises	45 seconds
Free Jumping	20–30 seconds
Isometric Exercises	30 seconds
Free Jumping	20–30 seconds

HEXAGON HUSTLE A large hexagon is formed using six cones. The student moves around the hexagon changing movement patterns every time he or she reaches one of the six points in the hexagon (Figure 5–25). On the teacher's command, the "hustle" stops and selected exercises are performed.

Instructional Procedures

1. To create a safer environment, children should move the same direction around the hexagon.
2. Laminated posters, with colorful illustrations, should be placed by the cones to inform children of the new movement to be performed.
3. Faster children should be encouraged to pass slower children on the outside.

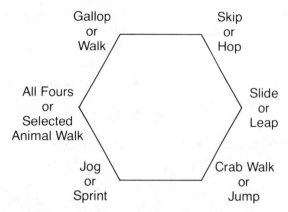

Figure 5–25 Example of Hexagon Hustle Activities

4. The direction of the "hustle" should be changed after every exercise segment.

Routine

Exercise	Repetitions or Time
Hustle	20–30 seconds
Push-Up from Knees	8–12 repetitions or 30 seconds
Hustle	20–30 seconds
Bend and Stretch (8 counts)	6–10 repetitions or 30 seconds
Hustle	20–30 seconds
Jumping Jacks (4 counts)	10–15 repetitions or 30 seconds
Hustle	30–40 seconds
Sit-Up (2 counts)	8–12 repetitions or 45 seconds
Hustle	30–40 seconds
Double-Leg Crab Kick (2 counts)	8–12 repetitions or 30 seconds
Hustle	20–30 seconds
Sit and Stretch (8 counts)	6–10 repetitions or 45 seconds
Hustle	10–20 seconds
Power Jumper	6–10 repetitions or 30 seconds
Hustle	10–20 seconds
Squat Thrust (4 counts)	6–10 repetitions or 45 seconds

Conclude Hexagon Hustle with relaxing exercises.

GRASS DRILLS/PARTNER RESISTANCE EXERCISES
Partner resistance exercises are a form of isometric exercise useful for developing strength. Since they have no aerobic benefits, partner resistance exercises should not be viewed as the only activities for a fitness module. Resistance exercises interspersed with vigorous activities can create the basis for a well-rounded fitness routine.

Instructional Hints

1. Exercises should be simple and enjoyable.

2. Children should be matched with a partner of about equal size and strength.

3. Exercises should be performed through the full range of motion at each joint.

4. The approximate duration of each exercise episode should be 8 to 12 seconds.

5. Signals should be used to start and stop the resistance exercise.

Suggested Partner Resistance Exercises

Arm curl: Exerciser keeps hands open with palms up and bends the arms at the elbows, keeping the upper arms against the sides. Partner places fists in the exerciser's palms. Exerciser tries to curl the forearms upward to the shoulders. To develop the opposite set of muscles, push down in the opposite direction, starting at the shoulder level.

Fist pull-apart: One partner places fists together in front of body at chest level (Figure 5–26). The other partner attempts to pull the hands apart while the first forces them together. To vary the exercise, one partner hold fists apart while the other tries to push them together.

Eagle: Exerciser stands with arms extended straight out to the sides. Partner holds exerciser's arms at the elbows. Exerciser tries to move arms down to the side of the body. Vary the exercise by having exerciser move the arms to an extended straight-above-head position or in front of the body.

Turtle shell: Exerciser is on hands and knees with head up. Partner pushes lightly on exerciser's back while exerciser attempts to curve the back like a turtle's shell.

Back stretcher: Exerciser spreads legs and bends forward at the waist with head up. Partner faces exerciser and places hands behind the exerciser's neck. Exerciser attempts to stand upright while partner pulls downward.

Leg stretcher: Exerciser lies on back with arms at side and legs extended. Partner straddles exerciser, placing feet alongside the ankles of the exerciser (Figure 5–27). Exerciser tries to spread legs. Vary the exercise by placing the partner inside the exerciser's legs and having the exerciser try to bring legs together.

Knee curl: Exerciser lies on stomach with legs straight, arms extended forward. Partner places hands on the back of the exerciser's ankles. Exerciser attempts to

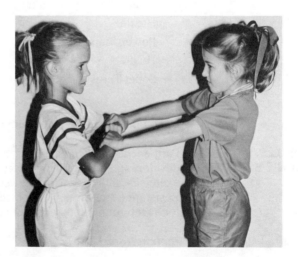

Figure 5–26 Fist Pull-Apart

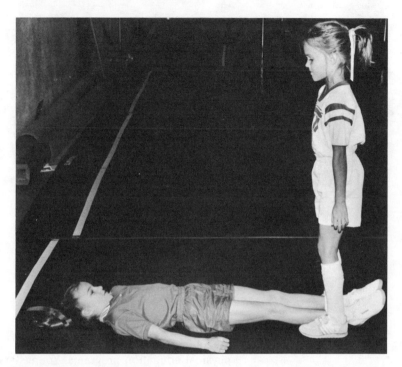

Figure 5-27 Leg Stretcher

bend the leg at the knee joint. Try in the opposite direction with knee joint beginning at a 90 degree angle.

Slow elevator: Exerciser assumes the down push-up position. The partner places hands on the upper back of the exerciser and applies minimal resistance as the exerciser completes a push-up.

A recommended companion activity for partner resistance exercises is Grass Drills—a strenuous routine in which the students move rapidly from a running-in-place position to a down position on the grass or floor. Grass Drills have the potential to provide the endurance benefits not received from partner resistance exercises.

Instructional Hints

1. The three basic positions are running in place, lying on the stomach, and lying on the back. Specific commands should be used to move students from one position to another (i.e. , "Go" signals running in place, "Front" signals moving to the prone position, and "Back" signals moving to a supine position).
2. Since the drills are executed in place, any type of formation is appropriate.
3. Varying the running in place movement (i.e., arms to the side, arms above head, heels to seat, etc.) increases interest.
4. Cardiovascular benefits can be increased by lengthening the running in place segment.

Routine

Exercise	Repetitions or Time
Grass Drills	20–30 seconds

Arm Curl (6–8 counts)	3–5 repetitions per partner
Grass Drills	20–30 seconds
Turtle Shell (6–8 counts)	3–5 repetitions per partner
Grass Drills	20–30 seconds
Fist Pull-Apart (6–8 counts)	3–5 repetitions per partner
Grass Drills	30–40 seconds
Leg Stretcher (6–8 counts)	3–5 repetitions per partner
Grass Drills	30–40 seconds
Sit-Ups	10–15 repetitions or 45 seconds
Eagle (6–8 counts)	3–5 repetitions per partner
Back Stretcher (6–8 counts)	3–5 repetitions per partner
Grass Drills	20–30 seconds
Slow Elevator (6–8 counts)	3–5 repetitions per partner
Grass Drills	10–20 seconds
Knee Curl (6–8 counts)	3–5 repetitions per partner

ROPE-JUMPING

Rope-jumping has become one of the more popular activities in elementary physical education programs. Youngsters throughout the country are quickly discovering that rope-jumping can be both challenging and fun. Due to its vigorous and continuous nature, rope-jumping also places demands on the cardiovascular system that can be sufficient to cause a training effect. While previously mentioned as a companion activity for selected exercises, a special section describing a progression of selected single rope-jumping activities can serve as the foundation of a number of additional fitness routines.

Suggested Rope-Jumping Activities

1. Jump in place to a specified rhythm (music, tom-tom) without using a rope.
2. Stretch the rope on the floor. Practice jumping back and forth over the rope.
3. Hold both ends of the rope in one hand and turn it so a steady rhythm can be made through a consistent turn. Just before the rope hits the floor, the jump should be made.
4. Holding the rope in both hands, swing the rope back and forth like a pendulum, jumping over the rope as it comes down toward the feet.
5. Start jumping the rope one turn at a time. Gradually increase the number of turns.
6. Introduce the two basic rhythms: slow time and fast time. Slow time is when the jumper takes a rebound step after the rope has been jumped. Fast time occurs when no rebound step is taken between jumps. Children should be encouraged to practice rope-jumping stunts in either slow or fast time.
7. Hop on one foot. This may be done continuously on one foot for a specified number of beats, then change to the other foot.
8. Combine hopping and jumping. Turn the body while jumping.
9. Stride jump. Assume a stride position with one foot in front of the other. Both feet should leave the floor simultaneously as the rope completes its downward motion. Vary the stunt by reversing the position of the feet during the jump.
10. Rocker step. Assume a stride position with one foot in front of the other. Swing the rope forward passing it first under the front foot while

rocking backward on the rear foot; then backward under the rear foot while rocking forward on the front foot.

11. Cross legs. As the rope passes under the feet, spread the legs in a straddle position to take the rebound. On the next pass of the rope, jump into the air and cross the feet to take the rebound.

12. Toe touch forward. Swing the right foot forward as the rope passes under the feet and touch the right toe on the floor. Alternate feet and touches.

13. Shuffling. Push off with the right foot and sidestep to the left as the rope passes under the feet. Repeat the step to the opposite direction.

14. Skier's jump. Stand on either side of a line on the floor. With feet together, jump from one side of the line to the other while the rope passes under the feet.

15. Heel click. Perform a heel click during the upward flight of the jump over the rope.

16. Foot circle. Holding both handles of the rope in one hand and bending forward, move the rope in a circular manner (parallel with the floor) passing it first under one foot and then the other.

17. Crossing arms. As the rope passes overhead beginning its downward path, cross the arms in front and jump the rope with arms crossed. Repeat, or practice crossing and uncrossing arms while jumping.

18. Double jump. A double jump is completed when the rope passes under the feet twice on the same jump.

SPORT-RELATED FITNESS ACTIVITIES

Many sport drills can be modified to increase the fitness demands placed on students. An advantage of sport-related fitness activities is that many children are highly motivated by sport activities. This may cause them to put forth a better fitness effort since they enjoy the activity. Thoughtful preplanning and creative thinking can result in drills that teach sport skills as well as provide fitness benefits. Following are some examples of fitness adaptations of sports skills.

Baseball/Softball

Base running: Set up several diamonds on a grass field. Space the class evenly around the base paths. On signal, they run to the next base, round the base, take a lead, then run to the next base. Faster runners may pass on the outside.

Most lead-up games: Children waiting on deck to bat and those in the field perform selected activities (skill or fitness related) while waiting for the batter to hit.

Position responsibility: Start children at various positions on the field. On command, children are free to quickly move to any other position. Upon reaching that position, the child is to display the movement most frequently practiced at that position (i.e., shortstop fields ball and throws to first base). Continue until all players have moved to each position.

Basketball

Dribbling: Each child has a basketball or playground ball. Assign one or more children to be "it." On command, everyone begins dribbling the ball and avoids being tagged by those who are "it." If tagged, that child becomes the new "it." A variation would be to begin the game by "its" not having a ball. Their objective would be to steal a ball from classmates.

Dribbling, passing, rebounding, shooting, and defense: Using the concept of a circuit, assign selected basketball skills to be performed at each station. Be sure there is ample equipment at each station to keep all youngsters active. Movement from one station to another should be vigorous and may include a stop for exercise.

Game play: Divide the class into four teams. Two teams take the court and play a game of basketball. The other teams assume a position along respective sidelines and practice a series of exercises. The playing and exercising teams change positions at the conclusion of the exercise sequence.

Football
Ball carrying: Divide the class into four to six squads. The first person in line carries the ball while zigzagging through preplaced boundary cones. The remainder of the squad performs a specific exercise. Upon completing the zigzag course, the first person hands off to the next person in line. This hand-off signifies a change in exercise for the remainder of the squad.

Punting: With partners, one child punts the ball to the other. After the receiver has the ball, the object is to see which child can get to his or her partner's starting position first. Repeat, with the receiver becoming the punter.

Forward passing: Divide the children into groups of no more than four. Children practice running pass patterns. Rotate the passing responsibility after every six throws.

Volleyball
Rotating: Place youngsters in the various court positions. Teach them the rotational sequence. As they reach a new court position, have them complete several repetitions of a specific exercise. On command, rotate to the next position. Select activities that enhance volleyball skill development.

Serving: Divide the class evenly among available volleyball courts. Starting with an equal number of children on each side of the net, begin practicing the serve. At the conclusion of each successful serve, the child runs around the net standard to the other side of the net, retrieves a ball, and serves.

Bumping and setting: Using the concept of the circuit, establish several stations to practice the bump and set. Movement from station to station should be vigorous and may contain a special stop for exercise.

Soccer
Dribbling: Working with a partner, have one child dribble the ball around the playground with the partner following close behind. On signal, reverse roles.

Passing and trapping: Working with partners or small groups, devise routines that keep the players moving continuously, i.e., jogging, running in place, performing selected exercises while waiting to trap and pass the soccer ball.

Game play: Divide the class into teams of three or four players per team. Organize the playground area to accommodate as many soccer fields as necessary to allow all teams to play. Make the fields as large as possible.

Routine

By combining sport skills with the principles of **FIT,** a wide variety of fitness routines can be developed. The following routine is an example of sport skills incorporated into an eight-station outdoor circuit:

Station 1, Soccer Dribble: Using only the feet, dribble the soccer ball to a predetermined point and back as many times as possible in the time provided.

Station 2, Basketball Chest Pass: With a partner, practice the chest pass. To place additional demands on the arm muscles, increase the distance of the pass.

Station 3, Football Lateral: Moving up and down the field, children practice lateraling the ball to one another.

Station 4, Softball Batting: Each child has a bat and practices proper swing technique. Be sure to allow ample space between hitters.

Station 5, Continuous Running Long Jump: Children take turns practicing the running long jump. After one child successfully completes a jump, the next one begins running down the runway. The activity should be continuous, with station members always moving.

Station 6, Soccer Inbounds Pass: With partners, practice the overhead inbounds pass. Keep the ball overhead and propel the ball forward with a flick of the wrist and proper arm motion.

Station 7, Field Hockey Passing: With partners, pass the field hockey ball back and forth between partners while moving up and down the field.

Station 8, Fielding a Softball: With partners, practice fielding a thrown ground ball. Make the activity more challenging by throwing the ball so the partner has to move to field the ball.

Exercises for Classroom Use

Since classrooms severely restrict the amount of movement students can generate, isometric exercises can be an excellent choice. Isometric exercises are characterized by having virtually no movement of the body part but a high degree of muscular tension. To prevent movement, the pulling, pushing, or twisting action is usually braced against some external force. This can be a desk, chair, wall, door frame, the floor, or a special isometric apparatus. Alternatively, one set of muscles can be worked against another, either individually or with a partner.

ISOMETRIC DESK EXERCISES

Many exercises can be done by children seated at their desks, with the desks used as braces. Maximum or near-maximum tension of the muscle group must be reached and held for approximately 8 seconds. Repetition of an exercise at any one session is not needed, because maximum development is gained from one contraction at an exercise session. Contractions should be performed at different joint angles to ensure strength development throughout the full range of movement.

Isometric exercises are presented in five categories: (1) abdominals, (2) arms, chest, and shoulders, (3) back, (4) legs, and (5) neck. In each case, the arms provide the stabilizing force for the specified development, so in a sense, all of the exercises benefit the arms and shoulders.

Abdominals

1. Sit straight against a backrest. Hold the edges of the chair with the hands. Pull the stomach in hard against the backrest.
2. Sit with hands (palms down, fingers extended) on the lower portion of the top of the thighs. Press down with the hands and up with the legs. (This exercise can also be done by placing the hands on the knees and lifting the straightened legs.)
3. Stand about 4 feet behind a chair. Bend forward at the waist until the hands can be put on the back of the chair (the elbows are straight). With a strong downward pull from the abdominal wall and the arms, pull down against the chair.

Arms, Chest, and Shoulders

1. Stand or sit. Clasp the fingers together in front of the chest with forearms held parallel to the floor (elbows out). Pull against the fingers to force the elbows out. Be sure to keep the chest up, the shoulders back, and the head erect.
2. Stand or sit. Using a grip with the palms together and the fingers interlocked (knuckles upward), push the palms together. Be sure the elbows are up and out.
3. Sit. Drop the hands, straight down, to the sides. Curl the fingers under the seat. Pull up with the shoulders, keeping the body erect.

4. Sit. Rest the thumb and near part of the hands on top of the chair seat. Push to raise the seat completely off the chair. Hold.

5. Stand or sit. With the left palm up and the right palm down, clasp the hands in front of the body, chest high. Press down with the right hand, resisting with the left. Reverse.

6. Sit. Grasp two books (with a total thickness of about an inch) in an opposed thumb grip. Squeeze hard with both hands.

7. Sit or stand. Put both hands on top of the head. Slide the hands toward the elbows so that each grasps an elbow. Raise the arms high and attempt to pull them apart while resisting with the hands on the elbows.

Back

1. Sit, bent forward and grasping the toes. Pull upward with the back while holding the toes.

2. Sit. Slide the hands forward to grasp the knees. From a slightly forward bend, pull back against the knee pressure. This exercise can also be done by placing the hands under the thighs near the knees.

3. Sit. Grasp the right hand under the chair. Apply pressure by leaning to the left. Reverse direction.

Legs

1. Sit with legs outstretched, the right ankle over the left. Press down with the right leg. Reverse position. Bend the knees and repeat right and left.

2. Sit, leaning forward. Cup the right hand around the outside of the left knee and vice versa. Force the knees outward against the inward pressure of the hands.

3. Sit, leaning forward. Place the cupped right hand against the inside of the left knee and vice versa. Force the knees together against the outward arm pressure.

Neck

1. Stand or sit. Clasp the hands behind the back of the head. Keeping the elbows well out, force the head back against the pressure of the hands.

2. Sit or stand. Place both hands flat against the forehead. Move the head forward against the pressure.

3. Sit or stand. Place the heel of the right hand against the head above the ear. Force the head to the right against the arm pressure. Repeat on the left side.

LIMITED-SPACE EXERCISES   Limited-space exercises involve movement and are useful for developing strength and aerobic capacity. The desks may have to be moved to the side of the room for maximum effectiveness. However, it is wise to continue fitness activities even when inclement weather prevents activities in larger spaces. Review the activities in the section entitled Exercises for Developing Fitness Routines (page 80). Activities that do not need much space can be adapted for the classroom. Following are examples of exercises that can be used:

Chair step-ups: Stand in front of the chair with the back away from the performer. Step up onto the chair with the right leg and bring the left leg onto the chair. Step down leading with the right leg. Repeat so that the left leg becomes the lead leg. Repeat 20 to 40 times on each leg.

Toe-ups: Using a walking-in-place motion, rotate up to the tiptoes. Swing the arms and walk quickly in place rising to the toes each time. Continue for 30 seconds to 1 minute.

Move in place: Perform a number of running, jumping, and hopping movements in place. Vary the activity by jumping in place and rotating the body back and forth with each jump. Try swinging a leg forward and backward while hopping. Mimic rope-jumping in place and swing the arms in proper rhythm. Continue for 30 seconds to 1 minute.

Inclined wall push-ups: See page 83 for a description of this activity. Perform as many as possible in 30 seconds.

Wall walk: Stand facing the wall with the feet shoulder width apart. Lean forward and place the hands on the wall. Walk the hands up and down the wall as far as possible. Continue for 30 seconds.

Rowing: See page 92 for a description of rowing. Exercises to strengthen the abdominal wall can always be done in the classroom.

Over the book: Place a book on the floor and hop or jump back and forth over it. Continue for 30 seconds to one minute.

Around the desk: Challenge students to see how many times they can move around their desk in 30 seconds. If space is limited, ask half the class to perform the activity while the remaining students are stretching. Reverse positions when time is up.

References

AAHPERD. (1988). *Physical Best Test Manual.* Reston VA: Author.

Corbin, C. B., & Lindsey, R. (1989). *Concepts of Physical Fitness with Laboratories.* Dubuque IA: Wm. C. Brown.

Dauer, V. P., & Pangrazi, R. P. (1989). *Dynamic Physical Education for Elementary School Children* (9th ed.). New York: Macmillan.

Pangrazi, R. P., & Dauer, V. P. (1989). *Lesson Plans for Dynamic Physical Education* (5th ed.). New York: Macmillan.